BORN IN SOUTH LA

100+ Remarkable African Americans Who Were Born, Raised, Lived or Died in South Los Angeles

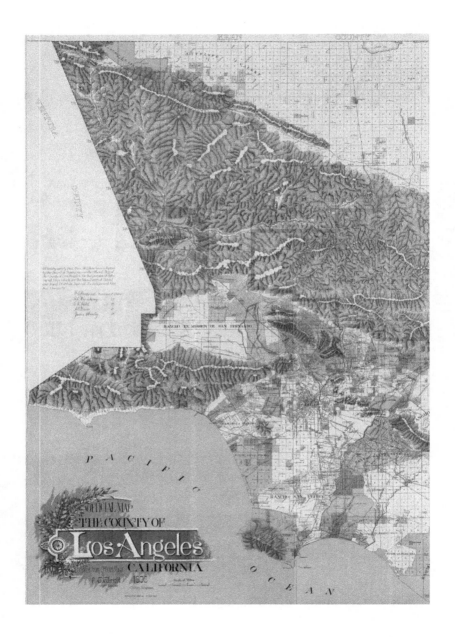

OFFICIAL MAP OF
THE COUNTY OF
Los Angeles
CALIFORNIA

BORN IN SOUTH LA

100+ Remarkable African Americans
Who Were Born, Raised, Lived or Died
in South Los Angeles

DR. RANDAL HENRY

GO CRENSHAW

The Crenshaw District, Los Angeles

Summary:

Born in South LA provides essential details on a range of remarkable achievements by African Americans from South LA in Architecture, Murals & Sculpting; Business; Classical Music, Dance & Opera; Education; Film & Television; Funk & Soul; Health, Public Safety & Science; Jazz & Blues; Journalism & Literature; Jurisprudence; Mythology & Fiction; Politics; Radio; Social Justice; Spirituality; and, Sports.

Notice:

The information in this book, referenced from available sources, is true to the best of our knowledge. However, the author and Go Crenshaw Publications disclaims all liability in connection with the use of this book.

First Printing 2022

ISBN 978-1-7361888-0-4 (hardcover)
ISBN 978-1-7361888-1-1 (paperback)
ISBN 978-1-7361888-2-8 (ebook)

Published by Go Crenshaw Publications
The Crenshaw District, Los Angeles, CA
www.gocrenshaw.com | www.gocrenshaw.shop

DEDICATION

This book is dedicated to people of South Los Angeles, California.

CONTENTS

PREFACE

Born in South LA was conceived from my desire to learn more about the amazing African Americans who have been born, raised, lived or died in South Los Angeles, California.

Prior to conducting the research that became this book, I used to wonder about the names of buildings and parks in South LA. I would wonder who Mariam Matthews was and why was her name on a library, who Maggie Hathaway was and why was her name on a golf course and who Norman O. Houston was and why was his name on a park. I came to realize that, although I was relatively well informed about Black History in general, I had a lot to learn about the notable accomplishments of African Americans who had been born, raised, lived or died in South LA.

As I completed my research, I realized that I had collected a trove of important details on a range of remarkable achievements by 100+ African Americans from South LA. I wrote this book to record what I've learned and to share it with others.

INTRODUCTION

Los Angeles, California is a special place for African Americans. In 1781, ten of the twenty-two adults who founded Los Angeles were of African or African-Latino descent—making LA the oldest and largest city in the U.S. founded by African people. From that time until today, Africans—and people of African descent—continue to make significant contributions to the growth and vibrancy of the City of Angels.

Born in South LA: 100+ Remarkable African Americans Who Were Born, Raised, Lived or Died in South LA documents the stories, struggles, accomplishments and events of some amazing people who have contributed to the community known as South LA. Spread over sixteen distinct chapters, *Born in South LA* provides essential details on a range of remarkable achievements by African Americans from South LA in the areas of Architecture; Murals & Sculpting; Business; Classical Music; Dance & Opera; Education; Film & Television; Funk & Soul; Health, Public Safety & Science; Jazz & Blues; Journalism & Literature; Jurisprudence; Mythology & Fiction; Politics; Radio; Social Justice; Spirituality and, Sports.

SOUTH LA'S OUTSTANDING ARTISTS

ASSEMBLAGE, ARCHITECTURE, MURALISM & SCULPTING

In Chapter One, we meet four outstanding artists: sculptor Beulah Woodard; assemblage artist John Outterbridge; architect Paul R. Williams; and muralist Richard Wyatt. We learn about each artist's relationship to South LA and how they used art to beautify public spaces, tell stories, create a sense of place, add character and represent afrocentricity in urban environments across LA County.

BEULAH WOODARD

FIRST AFRICAN AMERICAN ARTIST FEATURED IN LA COUNTY MUSEUM OF ART

(b. 1895 – d. 1955)

In 1935, Woodard, a sculptor, became the first African American artist honored with a solo exhibition at the LA County Museum of Art. Woodard began a lifelong interest in African culture at 12 years old. She specialized in African subjects, however Woodard's artistic media included clay, plaster, wood, copper, metal, oils, and papier-maché.

While at Polytechnic High, she began to explore sculpture and developed her art further with courses at the Los Angeles Art School, the Otis Art Institute, and the University of Southern California. As a member of the Association for the Study of African American Life and History, Woodard helped persuade LA's Mayor to enact LA's first Negro History Week. In 1937, she was the key organizer of the LA Negro Art Association. In 1950, Woodard helped establish the Eleven Associated Artist Gallery, a short-lived LA artist co-op that

included African American contemporaries such as Alice Taylor Gafford and William Pajaud and Chinese American artist Tyrus Wong.

Born in Ohio, at the age of 8 Woodard moved to LA with her family in 1903 and lived, created, contributed to, and died in South LA at age 60.

JOHN OUTTERBRIDGE

ASSEMBLAGE ARTIST, FORMER DIRECTOR OF THE WATTS TOWERS ARTS CENTER

(b. 1933 — d. 2020)

Known for his evocative sculptures made from found or discarded materials including cloth, containers and metal, John Outterbridge was a central figure in the Black assemblage arts movement and former director of the Watts Towers Arts Center. In the 1960s and 1970s, assemblage gave Black LA artists the chance to reclaim their community while calling out the indignities they faced.

In 1963, Outterbridge moved to LA, co-founded the Watts Towers Arts Center, and fathered the Black assemblage movement. Outterbridge and other artists including Betye Saar and Melvin Edwards were central figures in the movement and found inspiration for their work from the 1965 Watts rebellion. From 1969 to 1975, he directed the Communicative Arts Academy in Compton. In 2012, the California African American Museum honored Outterbridge with a lifetime achievement award alongside actor and director Sidney Poitier. Outterbridge's

art is in the collections of museums including the California African American Museum, the Los Angeles County Museum of Art, and the Museum of Modern Art in New York.

Born in Greenville, North Carolina, Outterbridge lived, served, created art, sustained artists and died in South LA.

PAUL R. WILLIAMS

FIRST LICENSED AFRICAN AMERICAN ARCHITECT IN CALIFORNIA

(b. 1894 – d. 1980)

Williams, a renowned African American architect—and one of the most successful and talented architects to practice in Los Angeles—is best known for the LAX theme building, Angelus Funeral Home, Perino's, the Ambassador and Beverly Hills Hotels, Saks 5th Avenue Beverly Hills, the Shrine Auditorium and numerous movie stars' homes.

In 1921, Williams became the first licensed African American Architect in California and the first certified African American architect west of the Mississippi. Williams designed over 2500 homes and commercial buildings, including those of numerous celebrities like Frank Sinatra, Lucille Ball, Desi Arnaz, and Lon Chaney. He also designed a number of important landmarks associated with the African American community—the First AME Church, the Second Baptist Church, the 28th Street YMCA, and the Angelus Funeral Home among them.

In 1923, Williams became the first Black architect to gain membership in the American Institute of Architects (AIA). In 1957 he was inducted as the AIA's first African American fellow. Williams childhood home at 1690 Victoria Avenue as designated Los Angeles Historic-Cultural Monument #170. Williams was born, raised, lived, and died in South LA.

RICHARD WYATT

LA'S MOST NOTED MURALIST

(b. 1955)

Wyatt showed artistic promise from an early age. When he was twelve, he won $200 at the first Watts Chalk-In, a sidewalk art contest sponsored by the Studio Watts Workshop. At the age of 17, his work was selected to be part of the Los Angeles County Museum of Art's 1972 "Panorama of Black Artists" exhibition, which garnered him widespread recognition and effectively launched his career as a member of the city's African American artistic community.

In 1978, after graduating from UCLA with a Bachelor of Fine Arts, Richard Wyatt began painting murals across the canvas of the City of Angels. One of the most noted muralists of Los Angeles, Wyatt's work often revolves around themes such as LA's history of multiculturalism.

Best known for his murals—like "James and Spectators" a now-faded mural that was part of the 1984 LA Olympic Games mural series, "Cecil" near the Watts Towers Art Center, and Nat King Cole on the iconic Capitol Records building in Hollywood, CA. Wyatt's work includes drawing, painting and public art installation.

Wyatt was born in Lynwood, California, and grew up in Compton before moving to the Crenshaw District in South LA.

SOUTH LA'S BUSINESS MOGULS

AN ENTREPRENEUR, PHILANTHROPIST AND REAL ESTATE TITAN

In Chapter Two, we meet three of South LA's most successful business leaders: LA's first African American millionaire, Bridget "Biddy" Mason; the leader of the largest African American owned business west of the Mississippi, Norman O. Houston; and, the wealthiest African American on the west coast, Robert Owens. Each used their business savvy to accumulate vast wealth and pursue philanthropic interests.

BRIDGET "BIDDY" MASON

FIRST AFRICAN AMERICAN MILLIONAIRE IN LA

(b. 1818 – d. 1891)

Bridget "Biddy" Mason was a woman of many talents. Although born into slavery, Mason was very intelligent and learned to read, write, nurse, sew and manage money. Ultimately, Mason's business acumen led to her becoming LA's first African American millionaire.

In 1855, Mason's slave owner brought her to LA hoping that California would become a slave state—it didn't so, he began preparing for a return trip to Salt Lake City, Utah a territory where slavery was legal. When Mason learned of his plans, she went into action. In 1856, understanding that slavery was illegal in California, Mason successfully petitioned a California Court for her freedom. She won, settled in LA as a free woman with her children and the rest, as they say, is history.

In 1866, just ten years later, Mason purchased a one-acre site near Broadway and Spring Street in downtown Los Angeles. In 1872, Mason helped found

South LA's famed First African Methodist Episcopal Church. After inheriting her accumulated wealth, her grandson (Robert Owen) became known as the wealthiest African American on the west coast. Mason's magnificent home has long since been demolished, however the Biddy Mason Memorial Park (333 S. Spring Street, LA 90013) honors her memory. Born in Georgia, Mason gained her freedom, lived her best life, and died in South LA.

NORMAN O. HOUSTON

PRESIDENT OF THE LARGEST AFRICAN AMERICAN-OWNED BUSINESS WEST OF THE MISSISSIPPI

(b. 1893 – d. 1989)

Norman O. Houston distinguished himself in the military, in the insurance field and in banking. Houston was drafted by the U.S. Army in 1918 and served as the regimental personnel adjutant with the 32nd division—the only African American to hold that position in the entire army.

In 1925, Houston joined the Golden State Mutual Life Insurance Company —the largest African American owned business west of the Mississippi River. Three years later, Houston was appointed to the position of company president. In 1947, Houston, by then one of LA's most prominent African American businessmen, helped organize Broadway Federal Savings and Loan and served as its chairman of the board for decades.

In 1976, Houston was appointed to the California State Athletic Commission where he became both the first African American on the commission and

the first to serve as chairman. Later, in 1976, then Los Angeles Mayor Sam Yorty appointed Houston to the, failed, 1976 Los Angeles Olympic Games Committee where he served admirably. Norman O. Houston Park (4800 S. La Brea Ave, LA 90008) honors his contributions to South LA.

Born in San Jose, CA, Houston lived, prospered, and died in South LA.

21

ROBERT OWENS

THE WEALTHIEST AFRICAN AMERICAN ON THE WEST COAST

(b. 1860 — d. Unknown)

Robert Owens, once the wealthiest African American on the west coast, was born with a silver spoon in his mouth. During his childhood, when his father died in 1882, Robert and his brother, Henry L., inherited their father's (Charles Owens) and mother's (Ellen Mason-Owens) real estate holdings including The Owens Livery Stable. Owens' grandmother, Bridget "Biddy" Mason, was widely known as LA's first African American millionaire. In 1891, when Robert inherited her estate, he constructed a new livery stable on her real estate holdings, as well as, a six-story building worth $250,000. Owens even purchased one of the most elegant homes in a predominantly white neighborhood. In addition, Owens owned a block of business buildings along LA's Spring Street that housed several prominent African American owned establishments bringing Robert even greater wealth.

Throughout the Progressive Era, Owens' social, political, and economic influence in Los Angeles made him one of the most powerful African American men in California and, by the start of the 20th century, Owens extensive property holdings made him one of the wealthiest African Americans on the west coast.

Owens was born, raised, lived and died in South LA.

SOUTH LA'S MASTERS OF THE CLASSICS

THE PRIMA BALLERINA, THE FIRST LADY OF GRAND OPERA, AND THE COMPOSER/CONDUCTOR EXTRAORDINAIRE

In Chapter Three, we meet three artists who were the first African Americans to achieve success and receive critical acclaim in their respective fields, the First Lady of the Grand Opera, Florence Cole Talbert; the technically stunning, amazingly graceful, barrier breaking, Prima Ballerina Janet Collins; and, the first African American to conduct a major American symphony orchestra, the Dean of African American classical composers, William Grant Still.

FLORENCE COLE TALBERT

THE FIRST LADY OF GRAND OPERA

(b. 1890 – d. 1961)

Madame Florence Cole-Talbert—an opera soprano, music educator, and musician—was called "The First Lady in Grand Opera" by the National Negro Opera Guild, was also one of the first African American women and opera artists performing abroad who received success and critical acclaim in classical and operatic music in the 20th Century. Most notably, she is credited with being the first African American woman to play the titular role of Verdi's "Aida" in a European staging of the opera.

Talbert was one of the first African American classical artists to record commercially. As a result of her career as a singer, a music educator, and

an active member of the National Association of Negro Musicians, she became a legendary figure within the African- American music community, also earning the titles of "Queen of the Concert Stage." A graduate of LA High School, Talbert, born in Detroit, raised and nurtured her talent in South LA.

JANET COLLINS

ONLY AFRICAN AMERICAN PRIMA BALLERINA FOR METROPOLITAN OPERA

(b. 1917 – d. 2003)

Janet Collins, the woman who broke the color barrier in the world of classical dance, opera and ballet in New York and most major U.S. and international cities—was also one of the few classically trained African American ballet dancers at a time when ballet trainers did not accept Black students.

Despite challenges, including facing outright racism and blatant discrimination, Collins performed in most of the major operas, including "Aida" and "Carmen," and became one of the greatest ballet dancers of her generation. By the age of 15, Collins had blossomed into a formidable talent and was asked to audition for a prestigious dance company. After being accepted, Collins declined the offer because they asked her to wear white face to disguise the fact that she was black.

More determined to succeed than ever, Collins vowed to perfect her art so that race would not be an issue. In 1940, Collins appeared in her first theatrical performance. In 1943, Collins co-starred with Katherine Dunham's troupe in the musical film "Stormy Weather." In 1951, Collins became the first and only African American prima ballerina for the New York Metropolitan Opera performing in a production of Aida. That year, Collins was recognized as the Best Dancer on Broadway and received the Donaldson Award for her performance in the Cole Porter play "Out of This World."

Born in New Orleans, Collins moved to LA with her family at the age of four, started taking dance classes in elementary school, graduated from Los Angeles City College, and went on to become the greatest prima ballerina of her era.

WILLIAM GRANT STILL

FIRST AFRICAN AMERICAN TO CONDUCT A MAJOR SYMPHONY

(b. 1895 – d. 1978)

Best known as the "Dean of African American composers", due to his close association with prominent African American literary and cultural figures, William Grant Still is considered part of the Harlem Renaissance movement.

Still was a pioneer in the following categories: the first African American to conduct a major American symphony orchestra; the first African American to have his own symphony performed by a leading orchestra; the first African American to conduct a major American orchestra in a performance of his own work; and, the first African American to conduct the orchestra for an opera performed on national television.

In 1931, Still's first major orchestral composition, Symphony No. 1 Afro-American, was conducted by Howard Hanson and performed by the Rochester Philharmonic Orchestra—marking the first time that a symphonic

score by an African American was performed by a white orchestra. By the end of World War II, the piece had been performed in Berlin, Chicago, London, Los Angeles, New York and Paris, and Symphony No.1 was recognized as the most popular symphony composed by an American.

In 1934, Still received his first Guggenheim Fellowship, started work on "Blue Steel", the first of his eight operas, and moved to Los Angeles. In 1936 Still conducted the Los Angeles Philharmonic Orchestra at the Hollywood Bowl and arranged music for films including: the 1936 "Pennies from Heaven" starring Bing Crosby and 1937's "Lost Horizon". Still was hired to arrange the music for the 1943 film 'Stormy Weather' but left the assignment because the movie studio (20th Century Fox) degraded African Americans in its movies.

In 1976, Still's home (1262 Victoria Ave, LA 90019) was designated Los Angeles Historic-Cultural Monument #169. The William Grant Still Art Center (2520 S. West View Street, LA 90016) is named in his honor. Born in Mississippi, Still, lived, composed, conducted and died in South LA.

SOUTH LA'S EDUCATIONAL PIONEERS

SCHOOL BOARD MEMBERS, TEACHERS, PRINCIPALS, A SUPERINTENDENT AND A PROFESSOR

In Chapter Four we meet six South LA educational pioneers: LAUSD School Boards champion of African American student achievement, Barbara Boudreaux; the first African American teacher and principal in Los Angeles public schools, Bessie Burke; the first African American to win a seat on the Los Angeles public school board and hold public office in California, Fay Allen; the first African American woman to serve as Superintendent of Los Angeles public schools, Michelle King; and, the high school music mentor of famous jazz musicians, Samuel Browne.

BARBARA BOUDREAUX

LA UNIFIED SCHOOL BOARD'S STAUNCHEST PROTECTOR OF AFRICAN AMERICAN STUDENT RIGHTS

(b. 1934)

Boudreaux, known as a strong and effective proponent of African American rights and a champion of African American student achievement, was elected to the LAUSD Board in 1991. She advocated for additional resources and programs for African American students to redress the decades of inequitable educational practices.

She also called for acknowledging Ebonics as a distinct language dialect, like other regional dialects, that should be taken into account when teaching

African American students. She noted this would require specialized training for all teachers who have contact with African American students. Boudreaux served two terms on the school board and had a fierce battle during the election campaign for a third term. Boudreaux was born, raised, and lives in South LA.

BESSIE BURKE

FIRST AFRICAN AMERICAN TEACHER & PRINCIPAL IN THE LA PUBLIC SCHOOL SYSTEM

(b. 1891 – d. 1968)

In 1911, trailblazing Bessie Burke was hired by the LA public school system, and became LA's first African American teacher. In 1918, she became LA schools' first African American principal, and—in 1938—LA's first African American principal to head a racially integrated school.

Burke retired from the LA Board of Education in 1955. She is remembered as a distinguished humanitarian and well-respected educator and administrator.

She served in many civic organizations including, the YWCA, Native California club, the NAACP, and Delta Sigma Theta Sorority, Inc. On March 17, 2009, Burke's home was included on the list of Historic Resources Associated with African Americans in Los Angeles, a place listed on the National Register of Historic Places. Burke, a graduate of the State Normal School—the precursor to UCLA—was born, raised, lived, and died in South LA.

FAY ALLEN

FIRST AFRICAN AMERICAN WOMAN TO HOLD PUBLIC OFFICE IN CALIFORNIA

(b. Unknown — d. Unknown)

In 1937, by competing for a seat on the Los Angeles public school board, Fay Allen became the first African American woman to run for public office in California. She lost but was not deterred. In 1939, Allen ran again and won making her the first African American woman to hold public office in California and the first African American on the Los Angeles public school board.

During her school board campaigns and during her time on the LA School Board, Allen was subject to significant racism. "A political column from May 8, 1939, commented on the election results in language that reflected the racial feelings of the period: Town full of squawks because Mrs. Fay Allen, a Negro music teacher, was elected to the Board of Education. Said squawks should be silenced. No intelligent person should complain because he voted for Mrs. Allen, not knowing her race. [...] Mrs. Allen is intelligent, traveled and experienced."

Allen advocated for standardization, revision and modernization of the school curriculum, an extension of education beyond the school age, and the election of school board members by district. Despite racial antagonism, Allen enjoyed widespread support from the teacher's union and other labor organizations.

Want Fay Allen On School Board

LOS ANGELES. Aug. 26—Democratic party groups and organized labor filed requests with the Board of Education this week asking that Mrs. Fay E. Allen, former board member, be appointed to the board as the result of a vacancy created by the resignation of John Dalton, who accepted the position of State Labor Commissioner.

Just prior to these liberal groups asking that Mrs. Allen be appointed to the board they had sharply criticized the board for not appointing Mrs. Allen to the vacancy caused by the resignation of Dr. E. Vincent Askey last May, shortly after the election in which Mrs. Allen was defeated by Mrs. Marie M. Adams, a nurse.

Among those requesting her appointment was the Teachers' union

Truly an unsung hero, Allen's date of birth, birthplace, and day of death are unknown, and despite her significant achievements, she somehow missed out on getting recognition of her place in California history. Allen lived in, and served the people of South LA.

GAIL E. WYATT

FIRST AFRICAN AMERICAN WOMAN LICENSED AS CLINICAL PSYCHOLOGIST IN CALIFORNIA

(b. 1944)

Wyatt, the first African American woman to be licensed as a psychologist in California, is a clinical psychologist, sex therapist, and professor in the Department of Psychiatry and Behavioral Sciences at UCLA.

At the time of publication, Dr. Wyatt was an Associate Director of the UCLA AIDS Institute and coordinated a core of behavioral scientists who conduct research who effectively incorporate socio-cultural factors into HIV/AIDS research. Dr. Wyatt has produced more than 110 journal articles and book chapters, and has co-edited or written five books, including *Stolen Women: Reclaiming our Sexuality, Taking Back Our Lives and No More Clueless Sex: 10 Secrets to a Sex Life That Works for Both of You.*

MICHELLE KING

FIRST AFRICAN AMERICAN WOMAN LAUSD SUPERINTENDENT

(b. 1961 — d. 2019)

In 2016, King became the Los Angeles Unified School District's first female superintendent and the first African American woman to serve as the LAUSD Superintendent. King spent her entire career in LAUSD, attending its schools and even working as a teacher's aide.

When she was promoted to superintendent, she said, "I want to be a role model for students who look like me." In 2017, King was selected as the National Association of School Superintendents, "Superintendent of the Year." King, a champion of unity and collaboration among all public schools, passed away at age 57 from cancer.

King said: "Sometimes in life, we don't think that certain positions are available to us particularly if you're a youth, a minority, that job or that position

or that role might not be for you because you don't see many role models, you don't see many folks in those positions," King said. "I feel that the appointment has said to particularly young women that anything is possible." King, a graduate of UCLA who received her doctorate in education from USC, was born, lived and grew up, and died in South LA.

SAMUEL BROWNE

HIGH SCHOOL MENTOR OF FAMOUS JAZZ MUSICIANS

(b. 1908 — d. 1991)

Samuel Rodney Browne, overcame the prejudice of his times and the challenges of a traditional music curriculum and—integrated the all-white faculty at Jefferson High School—becoming one of the first black teachers in the Los Angeles secondary school system at his alma mater.

Browne was subject to overt racism. He remembers being called into the office of an assistant district superintendent who cautioned him: "Remember, Brownie, now that you've got the job, you're going to have to do the work of three white men." He sometimes heard white teachers use racial slurs when talking about their black students. "I never forgot," he told the LA Times in a 1979 interview he gave in connection with a dinner held in his honor. "You carry that kind of a scar with you for life."

He prevailed upon the Board of Education to establish a class he called "Jazz Band" and—through it—subsequently helped educate and "pass" students who would later give birth to the modern or "Cool" school of jazz.

Browne was an accomplished pianist, organist, and choir director who was raised by a grandmother who made music lessons as important a part of his life as church.

He shined shoes and played the organ at various churches to pay his way through USC, where he earned bachelor's and master's degrees in music and education. Browne's major contribution to the LA music scene was in nurturing the talent of students, and future jazz luminaries such as Art Farmer, Buddy Collette, Don Cherry, Dexter Gordon, Horace Tapscott, OC Smith, and Roy Ayers.

Browne remained at Jefferson High until 1961, and died at home in South LA at the age of 85.

SOUTH LA'S STARS OF FILM AND TELEVISION

ACTORS, DIRECTORS AND FUNNY LADIES

In Chapter Five, we meet South LA's actors, actresses, and funny ladies. Among them are the very popular actress, Brenda Sykes; the first African American Female Academy Award nominee for Best Actress, the multi-talented Dorothy Dandridge; the talented, Baldwin Hills-raised and Stanford educated, producer, director and actor, Issa Rae; the first African American and youngest person nominated for an Oscar for best director, John Singleton; the successful African American film actress who broke through the traditional roles of "Maid" or "Servant Girl" to have a key character fully involved in a white movie, Louise Beavers; the woman who ran away from home to begin her film career with an uncredited role in D.W. Griffiths' 1915 *Birth of a Nation*, the pioneering African American film actress, Madame Sul-Te-Wan; former dancer, talented film and TV actress and preserver of the Historic Vision Theater in Leimert Park Village, Marla Gibbs; the first African American woman to star in a prime time television show, the bouncy and vibrant, Teresa Graves; and, the funny and attractive comedienne, Wendy Raquel Robinson.

BRENDA SYKES

SUCCESSFUL 1970'S BLAXPLOITATION FILM ACTRESS

(b. 1949)

In the early 1970's, during a time when there were very few African American women in leading lady roles on stage, on TV or on the big screen, actress Brenda Sykes was starring in blaxploitation film-era classics like The Liberation of L.B. Jones (1970), Skin Game (1971), Black Gunn (1973); Cleopatra Jones (1973), Mandingo (1975), and Drum (1976). Sykes also found success in mainstream films made for general audiences like the comedy Getting Straight (1970), Honky (1971), and Pretty Maids All in a Row (1971).

On the TV screen, Sykes appeared in One Life to Live (1968); Mayberry R.F.D., The New People, Room 222, and The Bold Ones (1969); The Doris Day Show and The Sheriff (1971); Love, American Style (1972); The Streets of San Francisco and Ozzie's Girls (1973); Young Love and Police Woman (1974); Harry O and Mobile One (1975); Executive Suite (1976-77); The Love Boat (1977); and, Good Time (1978).

Sykes, currently married to Paul Claude Hudson, and previously married to the pioneering hip-hop floetry artist Gil Scott-Heron from 1978 to 1987, was born in Louisiana, raised, educated and flowered as an actress in South LA.

DOROTHY DANDRIDGE

FIRST AFRICAN AMERICAN ACADEMY AWARD NOMINEE FOR BEST ACTRESS AND FIRST AFRICAN AMERICAN WOMAN FEATURED ON THE COVER OF A WHITE MAGAZINE

(b. 1922 — d. 1965)

Although her family lived in Watts, Dorothy Dandridge was a child film star. She appeared in Our Gang comedies (1935), and with The Dandridge Sisters in The Big Broadcast of 1936 (1936) and A Day at the Races (1937) with the Marx Brothers. She appeared in films throughout the 1940's and sang with the Count Basie Orchestra in Hit Parade of 1943 and with Louis Armstrong in Atlantic City (1944) and Pillow to Post (1945). In 1951, Dandridge returned to Hollywood to open the world famous Mocambo nightclub and was "discovered".

1954 was quite a year for Dorothy Dandridge. First, Dandridge's breakout performance as the star of Carmen Jones created a sensation, and she became the first African American to receive an Academy Award nomination for Best Actress. Next, in a move that shocked many a racist, Dandridge was featured on the cover of Life magazine, a white, mainstream periodical. Later in the

1950's, Dandridge received a Golden Globe Best Actress nomination for her work in Porgy and Bess.

Despite being recognized as one of the leading African American Actresses of her generation, Dandridge found it difficult to find acceptable roles in Hollywood. During the 1960's, she returned to the stage, recording studio and nightclub work that sustained her during the 1940's.

In 1984, Dandridge was awarded a star on the Hollywood Walk of Fame (north side of the 6700 block of Hollywood Blvd).

Despite the conclusion of The Los Angeles County Coroner's Office that Dandridge died of a fat embolism resulting from a right foot fracture sustained five days earlier, some allege that Dandridge died of an accidental drug overdose.

Born in Ohio, Dandridge lived and was raised in Watts, and attended McKinley Junior High School (now George Washington Carver Junior) in South LA.

ISSA RAE

ACTOR, CONTENT CREATOR, DIRECTOR, PRODUCER, WRITER

(b. 1985)

Issa Rae, born Jo-Issa Rae Diop, is one of the brightest breakout stars of the early twenty-first century.

In 2007, Rae graduated from Stanford University with a Bachelor of Arts in African and African American Studies. During her studies, Rae wrote, acted and directed and ultimately created the television show "Awkward Black Girl" which took off in 2011. After graduation, she received a fellowship from The Public Theater in New York City and took classes at the New York Film Academy. Since that time, Rae has received two Golden Globe Award nominations for Best Actress – Television Series Musical or Comedy and two Primetime Emmy Award nominations for Outstanding Lead Actress in a Comedy Series.

Unapologetically afro-centric, at the 2017 Emmy Awards, Rae told reporters, "I'm rooting for everybody black".

Rae, whose father hails from Senegal and whose mother is from Louisiana, was born in South LA, grew up in Baldwin Hills, graduated from King/Drew High School in Watts/Willowbrook and continues to live in South LA.

JOHN SINGLETON

FIRST AFRICAN AMERICAN AND YOUNGEST PERSON NOMINATED FOR "BEST DIRECTOR" OSCAR

(b. 1968 – d. 2019)

John Singleton was the first African American nominated for an 'Oscar' for Best Director by the Academy of Motion Picture Arts and Sciences. An actor, writer, director and producer, Singleton's masterpiece, "Boyz n the Hood," premiered in LA on July 2, 1991. Later that year, his screenplay was nominated for "Best Original Screenplay," and he was nominated for "Best Director" at the 64th Academy Awards, making him the youngest person and the first African American to be nominated for "Best Director."

Singleton made many films—among them, "Poetic Justice" (1993), "Higher Learning" (1995), "Rosewood" (1997), "Shaft" (2000), "Baby Boy"

(2001), "2 Fast 2 Furious" (2003), "Four Brothers" (2005), and his last film, "Abduction" (2011). Singleton also produced and directed a number of made-for-television-movies such as the documentary television film "L.A. Burning: The Riots 25 Years Later" (2016). Singleton struggled with hypertension and succumbed from a stroke. A 1990 graduate of USC, Singleton was born, raised, and died in South LA.

LOUISE BEAVERS

FIRST ACTOR TO BREAK THROUGH THE TRADITIONAL FILM ROLE OF BLACK SERVITUDE

(b. 1902 – d. 1962)

From the 1920's through the 1960's, Louise Beavers appeared in more than 160 films and dozens of TV shows. When Beavers started her career, African Americans in films were limited to acting in very few roles, usually as slaves or domestic help. Beavers, best remembered for her role as Delilah in the classic, Imitation of Life (1934), was one of the first African Americans to break through the traditional black role of servitude and/or comic relief by bringing more humanity to the screen, and the first African American actress whose character had a storyline equal to that of the film's white characters. Beavers most notable films include Bombshell (1933), Imitation of Life (1934), No

Time for Comedy (1940), Holiday Inn (1942) and Mr. Blandings Builds His Dream House (1948). Beavers' TV shows include Beulah (1952), The Danny Thomas Show (1953-1954), and The Magical World of Disney (1959-1960). In 1976, Beavers was posthumously inducted into the Black Filmmakers Hall of Fame.

Born in Cincinnati, Ohio, Beavers moved with her family to the LA area at age 11 and lived and died in LA.

MADAME SUL-TE-WAN

PIONEERING AFRICAN AMERICAN FILM ACTRESS

(b. 1873 – d. 1959)

In 1915, young Nellie Crawford, ran away from home, went to Hollywood, changed her name to Madame Sul-Te-Wan, and began her film career.

Sul-Te-Wan, known for the theatricality of her appearance, particularly her penchant for turbans and wearing her hair in two long braids, went on to appear in a number of high-profile classic films like D.W. Griffiths's Birth of a Nation (1915), the epic Intolerance (1916), Tarzan of the Apes (1918), The Lightning Rider (1924), King Kong (1933), In Old Chicago (1938), Safari (1940) and continued to act consistently throughout the 1940's and 1950's.

Although best known as a character actor, Sul-Te-Wan is noted for her memorable roles as Tituba in the Maid of Salem (1937) and in the Otto Preminger directed African American musical drama Carmen Jones (1954) where she appeared opposite Dorothy Dandridge as Hagar,

Dandridge's character's grandmother.

Madame Sul-Te-Wan was inducted in the Black Filmmakers Hall of Fame in 1986. Born in Louisville, Kentucky, Madame Sul-Te-Wan lived, flowered in South LA and died in Hollywood.

MARLA GIBBS

FAMOUS TV COMEDIENNE AND FORMER OWNER OF THE HISTORIC VISION THEATER

(b. 1931)

Since starting her career in 1968, comedienne Gibbs has appeared in more than 110 TV or film productions and received five nominations for the Primetime Emmy Award for Outstanding Supporting Actress in a Comedy Series. Gibbs is best known for her portrayal of the character Florence Johnston in the situational TV comedy The Jeffersons (1975–1985) and almost as well known for playing the role of Mary Jenkins in the TV series '227' (1985-1990). When dedicating her star (6840 Hollywood Boulevard) on the Hollywood Walk of Fame, the President of the Hollywood Chamber of Commerce said "Marla Gibbs has been recognized as one of the most beloved and talented actresses in the world. Her work is legendary".

From 1981 to 1999, Gibbs owned a jazz club on MLK Jr. Blvd In South Central LA called Marla's Memory Lane Jazz and Supper Club and the Historic Vision Theater in Leimert Park Village. Gibbs isa well-known for her acces-

sibility and for hanging out at festivals in the community the Pan-African Film Festival (PAFF.org) or the Leimert Park Village Book Fair. Although she was born in Chicago, through her ownership of property, (e.g. Historic Vision Theater and Marla's Memory Lane) and preservation of historic spaces, Gibbs made significant contributions to life in South LA.

TERESA GRAVES

FIRST AFRICAN AMERICAN ACTRESS TO STAR ON TV DRAMA SERIES

(b. 1948 – d. 2002)

From 1969 through 1975, Teresa Graves, a bouncy, beautiful and talented actress and singer, landed many acting roles on a number of TV shows including The Funny Side (1971); the very popular TV show, Rowan & Martin's Laugh-In where became a regular (1969-1971); and, The New Dick Van Dyke Show (1972). Graves also appeared in several films including That Man Bolt (1973) and Black Eye (1974).

Graves is best known for her starring role as the undercover police detective Christie Love in the mid-70's TV crime-drama Get Christie Love! (1974-

1975) when she became the second African American woman to star in her own hour–long TV series (See Hadda Brooks pg. 76) and the first to star in a TV drama series. More recently, Graves was featured in the 2013 hit "Keeping Up with the Joneses". Born in Houston, Graves was raised, educated, lived in Hyde Park where she cared for her mother and died in South LA

WENDY RAQUEL ROBINSON

AWARD-WINNING COMEDIENNE AND ANIMATION ACTRESS

(b. 1967)

Since starting in 1992, Wendy Raquel Robinson, one of today's most success-ful and talented comedians, has accumulated over 75 acting credits. HBCU educated, Robinson earned her Bachelor of Fine Arts degree from Howard University and went to work. Robinson first appeared on the "Martin" show in 1993 starring Martin Lawrence and she has been steadily going strong since appearing on shows such as "The Sinbad Show"; and the "Steve Harvey Show". In the world of animation, over the years, Robinson has voiced characters on cartoon shows like "The Proud Family", "The Boondocks" and "Family Guy". Robinson is a recurring star on TV shows like "Grey's anatomy"; "Dear White people"; and Issa Rae's "Insecure". Robinson is best known for her portrayal of Regina 'Piggy' Grier on The Steve Harvey Show (1996-2002). To her credit as a 'funny lady', almost every year, from 2000 through 2015, Robinson was

nominated for an NAACP Image Award, finally winning the award for 'Outstanding Actress in a Comedy Series' in 2014 for her work in the TV series "The Game".

Robinson, of African American and Native American heritage, was born in South LA.

SOUTH LA'S FUNK & SOUL STARS

THE PRINCE OF MOTOWN, A RAPPER, SOUL BAND, VIBRAPHONIST, MULTI-INSTRUMENTALIST AND TWO ANGELIC SINGERS

In Chapter Six we meet a rapper, funksters and soul stars like the leader of the hottest soul band of the 1960's and 70's, Charles Wright of the Watts 103rd Street Rhythm Band; one of the most successful dance artists, and cross-over music icons of the 80's, Soul Train's own, Jody Watley; vocalist, writer, producer of "What's Going On"—a classic ranked as the greatest album of all time, the socially conscious soul singer, Marvin Gaye; the amazing five-octave soprano singer whose career was cut short by breast cancer, Minnie Riperton; a superstar in her own right, the 'destined for stardom-at-birth daughter' of the all-time great pianist/vocalist, Nat King Cole, the midas-touched—red hot in the 1970's—singer Natalie Cole; artist, businessman, community-builder, father, husband, "rapper/hip-hop-preneur", Nipsey Hussle; producer, instrumentalist, singer, producer, and Director of the Grammy Music Awards show, Patrice Rushen; and the musical pioneer and creator of a funky jazz-hop fusion, vibraphonist Roy Ayers.

CHARLES WRIGHT

FOUNDER OF CHARLES WRIGHT AND THE WATTS 103RD STREET RHYTHM BAND

(b. 1940)

Singer, songwriter, and multi-instrumentalist Charles Wright made his way to Watts in 1950. In 1962, Wright began recruiting the 8-member band and, around the time of the Watts Riots, founded Charles Wright and the Watts 103rd Street Band. In the process, Wright formed what would become one of the most quintessential Soul and Funk Bands of the late '60s and early '70s.

Wright and the Watts 103rd Street Rhythm Band top singles include "Do Your Thing"; "Love Land"; and "Express Yourself". "Express Yourself" was sampled by Los Angeles rap group N.W.A 1988 and has been used in over fifty film and

video game soundtracks, including Straight Outta Compton (2015), Mr. & Mrs. Smith, (2005), Remember the Titans (2000), and Boogie Nights (1997), plus numerous TV shows and TV commercials around the English speaking world. Born in Mississippi, Charles Wright continues to do his thang, express himself and live in South LA.

JODY WATLEY

MUSICAL ICON AND GENRE CROSSING DANCER, SINGER, SONGWRITER, ARTIST, AND PRODUCER

(b. 1959)

Jody Watley began her music career dancing on "Don Cornelius" Soul Train TV show while attending Dorsey High. In 1977, she became a member of the musical group "Shalimar" and stayed with them until 1983. Watley has won a host of awards including Soul Train Music Awards, MTV Video Music Awards, and American Music Awards.

In 1987 Jody Watley won a Grammy for Best New Recording Artist, and was nominated for Best Female R&B Performance. In 2008, she was the recipient of a Lifetime Achievement Award from Billboard magazine, and was also prominently featured in the historic black issue of Vogue Italia.

In December 2016 Billboard ranked her as the 21st most successful dance artist of all time. In 2017, the "Black Music Honors TV" special recognized

Watley as "Crossover Music Icon Honoree" for her groundbreaking achievements and influence. In 2018, Billboard ranked Watley as among one of the top female artists of all time (i.e., # 53). Born in Chicago, Watson was raised, got on Don Cornelius' Soul Train as a Dorsey High School student, and flowered as a creative artist in South LA.

MARVIN GAYE

THE "PRINCE OF MOTOWN" AND PRODUCER AND ARTIST OF "THE GREATEST MUSICAL ALBUM OF ALL-TIME"

(b. 1939 — d. 1984)

One of the greatest singers, song writers, record producers, and visionaries of all time, Marvin Gaye, the son of a minister, started singing in the Pentecostal church with his father accompanying him on piano when he was but four years old. Gaye's Motown hits include "Ain't That Peculiar," "How Sweet It Is (To Be Loved By You)," and "I Heard It Through the Grapevine."

Gaye also recorded duets with Mary Wells, Kim Weston, Tammi Terrell, and Diana Ross. During the 1970s, Gaye recorded the albums "What's Going On," and "Let's Get It On."—becoming one of the first artists in Motown to break away from the strict reins of that recording company. Gaye's album "What's Going On" was listed as the greatest album of all time on the 2020 Rolling Stone list of the 500 greatest albums.

Gaye, one of the most socially conscious soul singers, was born in Washington DC, lived and, on April 1, 1984, the day before his 45th birthday. After an argument, he was shot dead by his father, Marvin Gaye Sr., at their house in the West Adams neighborhood of South LA.

MINNIE RIPERTON

AMAZING FIVE-OCTAVE SOPRANO SINGER AND PIONEERING BREAST CANCER WARRIOR

(b. 1947 — d. 1979)

Possessor of a simply mesmerizing voice—and one of the first celebrities to go public with a breast cancer diagnosis—singer-songwriter Minnie Riperton is perhaps best known for her five-octave soprano range, her 1975 hit single "Lovin' You" from her 1974 gold album titled "Perfect Angel."

Riperton's 1970 debut solo album 'Come to My Garden' is now considered a masterpiece. On June 7, 2009, US TV network's TV One channel premièred a one-hour documentary on Riperton's career and life. In 1977, Riperton

became a spokesperson for the American Cancer Society, and in 1978, received the society's Courage Award, which was presented to her at the White House by, then, President Jimmy Carter. Born in Chicago, Riperton lived, and died of breast cancer at age 31, in South LA.

NATALIE COLE

SINGING SUPERSTAR OF THE 1980'S AND DAUGHTER OF NAT KING COLE

(b. 1950 — d. 2015)

As the first female artist to have two platinum albums in one year and star in her own TV special—Natalie Cole was red-hot in the 1970's. Daughter of Maria Hawkins Ellington, a former singer with the Duke Ellington Orchestra, and singer icon and pianist extraordinaire, Nat King Cole. Her "destined-for-stardom-at-birth" promise was realized success rose rapidly in the late 1970s with smash hits such as "This Will Be," "Inseparable," and "Our Love."

In early 1979, Cole was awarded a star on the Hollywood Walk of Fame. In 1991, singing songs her famous father recorded nearly 30 years earlier, Cole released her best-selling album "Unforgettable...with Love," eventually winning several Grammy Musical Awards, including Album of the Year, Record of the Year, and Best Traditional Pop Vocal Performance for the top song. Cole was born, lived, and died in South LA.

NIPSEY HUSSLE

ARTIST, BUSINESSMAN, COMMUNITY BUILDER, ENTREPRENEUR

(b. 1985 — d. 2019)

Ermias Joseph Asghedom, aka Nipsey Hussle, became known for his numerous mixtapes, including his "Bullets Ain't Got No Name" series, "The Marathon," "The Marathon Continues,' and "Crenshaw."

Nipsey's mother was African American, and his father was an Eritrean immigrant. Hussle credits a three-month trip to Eritrea in East Africa with his father and his brother with inspiring him to become a community activist and hip-hop-traneur. Hussle's debut studio album, "Victory Lap," was released in 2018 to critical acclaim and commercial success, and was nominated

for the Best Rap Album at the 61st Grammy Awards in 2019. Hussle was shot and killed in the parking lot of a strip mall he owned, just off Crenshaw Blvd, in South Los Angeles on March 13, 2019. He was loved for his hip-hop entrepreneurism, and for being down to earth. Hussle was born, raised, and died in the Crenshaw district of South LA.

PATRICE RUSHEN

VOCALIST, MULTI-INSTRUMENTALIST, COMPOSER, DIRECTOR, AND PRODUCER

(b. 1954)

Artist, producer, and musical director, pioneering Patrice Rushen was the first woman to serve as musical director of the NAACP Image Awards, an honor she held for twelve consecutive years. Also, she is the only woman who has been the musical director/composer for the People's Choice Awards and HBO's Comic Relief. In addition, Rushen was the only woman who served as musical director/conductor/arranger for a late-night television talk show.

As a recording artist with multi-Grammy nominations for songs such as "Forget Me Nots'" in 1982, "Men in Black" in 1997, and "Signature" in 1998. She has fourteen solo albums to her credit. The first woman to serve as the head composer/musical director for the Emmy Awards and as musical director for the 46th, 47th & 48th Annual Grammy Awards. Patrice Rushen was born and raised in South LA.

ROY AYERS

COMPOSER, PRODUCER, VIBRAPHONIST & JAZZ-FUNK PIONEER

(b. 1940)

Son of a trombonist and a piano-playing mother, Roy Ayers was given his first pair of vibraphone mallets by the legendary African/Black American vibraphonist, Lionel Hampton. Ayers grew up in the LA hotbed known as the Central Avenue jazz scene. He played in several bands growing up, and formed his own band, Roy Ayers Ubiquity, in the mid-1970's.

"The Godfather of Neo Soul," Roy Ayers is best known for his hits "Everybody Loves The Sunshine," "Searchin," and "Running Away." In 1973, he wrote the highly regarded soundtrack to "Coffy," a blaxploitation film starring Pam Grier. In 1976, he released the classic album "Everybody Loves the Sunshine."

In 1977 he recorded his biggest hit 'Running Away,' and in 1979 he scored a top ten Billboard chart single with "Don't Stop the Feeling."

A documentary film featuring Ayers titled the "Roy Ayers Project'" reviews his musical development, the scope of his influence, and hip-hop artists who've sampled his music. Ayers was born, raised, and graduated from Jefferson High School, and lives in South LA.

SOUTH LA'S LEADERS IN HEALTH, HOUSING AND PUBLIC SAFETY

A FIREMAN, A POLICE OFFICER, DOCTORS, DENTISTS, POLICE COMMISSIONERS AND A HOUSING ADVOCATE

In Chapter Seven we meet leaders of health, public safety and science from South LA such as the following: the first African American firefighter to be promoted to the position of lieutenant within the segregated Los Angeles Fire Department, George W. Bright; the social worker who became LA's first African American Female Police Officer, Georgia Ann Robinson; an early advocate for housing, the first African American on LA Housing Commission and the first to manage an LA City Housing project, Jessie L. Terry; the first African/Black American graduate of the USC Dental School, the first licensed oral surgeon and the first appointed to the LA Police Commission, John Somerville; the first African American to graduate from the University of California School of Medicine, and the first hired by the LA County Health Department, Leonard Stovall; the first African American woman, and second Black on the LAPD Board of Commissioners, Marguerite Justice; a pioneer in free and afford-able health care clinics, the first African American woman doctor in LA, Ruth Janetta Temple; LA's first African American firefighter and the first to die in the line of duty, Sam Haskins; the first African American woman to graduate from the USC School of Dentistry, and the second in California to receive a Doctor of Dental Surgery degree, Vada Somerville.

GEORGE W. BRIGHT

FIRST AFRICAN AMERICAN PROMOTED WITHIN THE LOS ANGELES FIRE DEPARTMENT

(b. 1862 – d. Unknown)

Bright, for decades erroneously recorded as the first African American firefighter in LA, was actually the second. Sam Haskins was the first. Bright became the second African American volunteer member of the LA Fire Department on October 2, 1897. Later, he was appointed by the Fire Commission as a call-man and assigned to Engine Co. No. 6 in South Central LA and rapidly promoted to a full-time hose-man and assigned to Engine Co. No. 3. On January 31, 1900 He was promoted to Driver Third Class and assigned to Chemical Engine Co. No. 1.

Before the commission would certify his promotions, Bright, as the first African American to apply for such advancement, was required to go to the Second

Baptist Church and obtain an endorsement from his minister and congregation. To avoid Bright supervising white firefighters, the department gathered all of the department's African Americans and formed LA's first all-Black fire company. Bright retired in 1917 Los Angeles Fire Department continued segregating Firemen until the 1950's. Bright's birthplace is unknown, but he lived and served in South LA.

GEORGIA ANN ROBINSON

FIRST AFRICAN AMERICAN FEMALE POLICE OFFICER WITH THE LOS ANGELES POLICE DEPARTMENT

(b. 1879 – d. 1961)

In 1916, at the age of 37, after having previously been active in community affairs and social work, Georgia Ann Robinson became the first volunteer African American female officer with the Los Angeles Police Department. Three years later, in 1919, she was appointed an officer and became the first African American woman to be selected to join the LAPD—and possibly the first black woman on a police force anywhere in the United States of America.

Officer Robinson worked on juvenile and homicide cases, including referring women and girls to social agencies, inspiring her to found the Sojourner Truth

Home, a shelter for women and girls. Robinson's police career ended at the age of 49 when she permanently lost her sight after being injured by a prisoner. When asked she said "I have no regrets. I didn't need my eyes any longer. I had seen all there was to see." Born in Louisiana, Robinson lived, worked—made history—and died in South LA.

JESSIE LOUISE TERRY

FIRST AFRICAN AMERICAN APPOINTED TO LA HOUSING COMMISSION, FIRST AFRICAN AMERICAN CHAIRPERSON OF LA HOUSING COMMISSION AND LA'S FIRST FEMALE HOUSING PROJECT MANAGER

(b. 1885 – d. 1979)

On June 21, 1939, Jessie Louise Terry, an early leader in the field of Housing, became the first African American appointed to the LA Housing Commission. Later, Terry was elected Chairperson of the commission, serving in the role through January 6, 1944. Under Terry's leadership, bending rules that were designed to foster segregation, the housing commission began advocating for the city to create integrated housing projects. In 1943, again under Terry's guidance, the housing commission rescinded policy of using racial quotas and based housing decisions based on the needs of the existing population in the community. According to the National Committee Against Discrimination in Housing, once Terry's anti-segregationist policies had been established, Los Angeles was said to have "the most enlightened, liberal and complete interracial policy to be effected anywhere in public housing".

After her term on the commission was up, Terry went on to become LA's first African American and first woman to manage an LA city housing project. Active in civic organizations, Terry also helped found the first African American YMCA Branch in LA and the LA Chapter of the National Organization of Negro Women. The Jessie L Terry Senior Housing Manor (3100 Vermont Ave, LA 90007) is named in her honor. While her birthplace has been lost to history, Terry lived, served and died in South LA.

JOHN SOMERVILLE

FIRST AFRICAN AMERICAN TO GRADUATE AS DOCTOR OF DENTISTRY AT USC AND FIRST AFRICAN AMERICAN APPOINTED TO LOS ANGELES POLICE COMMISSION

(b. 1881 – d. 1973)

In 1903, Somerville became the first African American to enter—and later—graduate from the School of Dentistry at USC. Responding to Jim-Crow-era laws and segregation, Somerville said, "I made this resolution—that I would work at any job that I could find, no matter how menial, until I saved enough money to enter an institution of higher learning to prepare myself for a trade or profession. I wanted to earn a place where I would not have to ask any other fellow for a job."

After working for more than a year and saving money for dental school, Somerville enrolled at USC. While in school, he met and married fellow USC dental school student, Vada Watson who became the first African American woman to earn a USC Doctorate of Dentistry. The Somerville's thrived. In 1914 the Somerville home hosted NAACP meetings including the formation of the first LA NAACP branch. In 1928, John and Vada opened the Somerville Hotel—the principal African American enterprise on LA's thriving Central Avenue. The Somerville's sold the hotel to repay debts incurred during the Great Depression and the new owners renamed it—the Dunbar Hotel. In 1936, Somerville

became the first African American to be named "delegate" to the California Democratic Convention. In 1949, he was appointed to the Los Angeles Police Commission becoming the first African American named to a law enforcement oversight commission in California. Born in Jamaica, Somerville lived, married, practiced dentistry, enriched the community, and died in South LA.

LEONARD STOVALL

FIRST AFRICAN AMERICAN GRADUATE OF UNIVERSITY OF CALIFORNIA MEDICAL SCHOOL

(b. 1887 – d. 1956)

In 1912, Stovall became the first African American graduate of the University of California Medical school and the first African American medical doctor to join the staff at LA County's General Hospital. He conducted a study of tuberculosis in LA's African American community and established a clinic providing low-cost medical services to the community.

In 1933, realizing the need for health education, and recognizing that there were practically no hospitals in Los Angeles that would admit and treat African Americans for tuberculosis, Stovall established a 50-bed hospital

and founded the Outdoor Life and Health Association for patients of all races suffering from tuberculosis in Duarte, California. In 1940, the organization opened a sanatorium and was renamed the Stovall Foundation. His son, Gerald Stovall also became a medical doctor. Born in Georgia, both Stovall's lived, served through the practice of medicine, and died in South LA.

MARGUERITE JUSTICE

FIRST AFRICAN AMERICAN WOMAN APPOINTED TO LOS ANGELES POLICE COMMISSION

(b. 1921 — d. 2009)

In 1971, Justice became the first African American woman, and the second woman, to serve as a police commissioner in the United States. Justice, a long-time South LA community activist fondly referred to as "Mama J," was appointed by Mayor Sam Yorty to a two-year term on the five-member LA Police Commission. Asked how she hoped to attune her own sensitivities to law-and-order problems particular to minority communities, Justice answered: "I'm black. Therefore, my sensitivities already extend to minorities. I'm not rich and so my sensitivities also extend to the poor and oppressed."

In Memory of
Marguerite Justice
July 21, 1921 - September 17, 2009

Justice also served as a board member of the Los Angeles Community Redevelopment Agency. In 2004, Justice received the Police Historical Society's Jack Webb Award for her sustained commitment to law enforcement. Born in New Orleans, Mama J' Justice moved to California in 1945 and lived, served, and died in South LA.

RUTH JANETTA TEMPLE

FIRST AFRICAN AMERICAN WOMAN DOCTOR IN LA

(b. 1892 – d. 1984)

Free, affordable health clinic pioneer and provider of healthcare and education to underserved communities in South LA, Dr. Ruth Janetta Temple was
a true public health innovator. In 1913, Temple enrolled in the College of
Medical Evangelists (now Loma Linda University) and, in 1918, became the
first African American woman to graduate from this institution. Temple's
family could not afford to fund her college education, but the Los Angeles
Forum, a black men's civic organization, arranged to pay Temple's tuition.
Upon graduation from Loma Linda, Temple began working to create public
health services for underserved low-income communities in Los Angeles so
she and her husband Otis Banks turned their newly purchased five-bedroom
bungalow into the Temple Health Institute, a free medical clinic that discussed
common community issues such as substance abuse, immunization, nutrition
and sex education and the first of its kind in all of LA. After over twenty years
of service in the medical profession, Temple was accepted in the Public Health

master's program at Yale University in
1941, and the Los Angeles City Health
Department awarded her with a scholarship to support her advanced educational endeavors. The Dr. Ruth Temple
Health Care Center located at 3834 S
Western Ave, LA 90062 is named in her
honor.

Born in Natchez Mississippi, Temple
was raised, served and excelled in
South LA.

SAM HASKINS

LA'S FIRST AFRICAN AMERICAN FIREFIGHTER AND FIRST AFRICAN AMERICAN FIREFIGHTER TO DIE IN THE LINE OF DUTY

(b. 1855 – d. 1895)

The first African American volunteer firefighter in the city, Sam Haskins had arrived in Los Angeles about 1880. Back then, being a volunteer firefighter was very prestigious, so it was surprising that a Black person would have had the means to join the department back then because they had to buy their own equipment and clothes.

On the cool evening of Nov. 19, 1895, Haskins responded to a 6 p.m. alarm, taking his position on the back of the wagon hauling the steam pump. With the station's mascot, Chief the dog, in the lead, the horse-drawn wagons raced

along 1st Street, which was riddled with potholes and streetcar tracks, toward Main. When the wagon Haskins was standing on hit a bump, he lost his balance and fell between the wheel and the pump. It took firefighters and passersby more than 10 minutes to take off the wheel to free him. They took him back to the firehouse, where he died a few minutes later. Born a slave in Virginia in 1855, Haskins died in 1895 in the line of duty in South LA.

VADA SOMERVILLE

FIRST AFRICAN AMERICAN WOMAN DOCTOR OF DENTISTRY AT USC

(b. 1885 – d. 1972)

In 1918, Somerville became the first African American Woman Doctor of Dentistry at USC and the second African American woman in California to receive a Doctor of Dental Surgery degree. Married to John Somerville, USC's first African American Dentist. They practiced dentistry together until 1933 when Vada retired and became the leading light in the city's civic and community organizations, serving on the executive boards of such groups as the Los Angeles League of Women Voters, the Council on Public Affairs, UCLA's YWCA, and the USC Half Century Club.

Together, John and Vada Somerville built the Somerville Hotel, lost it during the Great Depression, and it was later renamed the Dunbar Hotel. Born in

Pomona, Somerville was educated at USC and lived, married, practiced dentistry, and died in South LA.

SOUTH LA'S JAZZ AND BLUES GIANTS

SINGERS, PIANISTS, SAXOPHONISTS, A HIPSTER, A BASSIST AND A TROMBONIST

In Chapter Eight, we meet South LA's jazz and blues masters such as jazz bass master—and the man considered to be one of the greatest musical compos-ers of all-time—Charles Mingus Jr; one of South LA's several masters of the tenor saxophone, and the only jazz artist academy nominee for the Best Actor in a motion picture award, Dexter Gordon; the first" female jazz saxophonist to play with the top jazz bands of the day, Elvira "Vi" Redd; the greatest modern blues singer and one of the greatest and most soulful vocal artists of all-time, Etta James; the ragtime pianist from New Orleans, band leader and the first composer of jazz music, Ferdinand "Jelly Roll "Morton; California's best kept jazz secret, orchestra leader and National Endowment for the Arts Jazz Master, Gerald Wilson; pianist, vocalist, composer and Queen of the Boogie, the captivating Hadda Brooks; South LA's self-taught son of a preacher, legendary jazz pianist and bebop memoirist, Hampton Hawes; Duke Ellington's best known singer, most musical female vocalist in the Band and operator of Ivie's Chicken Shack, Ms. Ivie Anderson; the ultimate OG jazz hipster, friend to Billie Holiday, master of the tenor sax and populizer of the all things 'Cool', the standard-setting, Lester Young; and, the pioneering female jazz trombonist, composer and arranger, Melba Liston.

CHARLES MINGUS

ONE OF THE GREATEST JAZZ MUSICIANS AND COMPOSERS IN HISTORY

(b. 1922 – d. 1979)

Virtuoso bass-player, accomplished pianist, composer, arranger, and bandleader, Charles Mingus has been recognized as one of the greatest jazz musicians and composers in history. In the 1940's, Mingus played with Louis Armstrong, Kid Ory, Les Hite, and Lester Young.

Ultimately, Mingus formed his own publishing company and recording company to protect and document his original music. Mingus, a uniquely iconoclastic figure, cut a path through jazz in the middle of the 20th century, creating a musical and cultural legacy that became universally lauded. In 1993, the United States Library of Congress acquired Mingus's collected papers—

including scores, sound recordings, correspondence, and photos—in what they described as "the most important acquisition of a manuscript collection relating to jazz in the Library's history." Beneath the Underdog: His World, Mingus' autobiography was first published in 1971 by Alfred A. Knopf. Born in Arizona, Mingus was raised in Watts and attended Jordan High in South LA.

DEXTER GORDON

JAZZ MASTER AND THE ONLY MUSICIAN NOMINATED FOR AN ACADEMY AWARD FOR BEST ACTOR

(b. 1923 — d. 1990)

Acclaimed as a National Endowment of the Arts Jazz master in 1986, Dexter Gordon was second in the pantheon of great tenor saxophonists—behind only Lester Young—in the 'bebop' era. Gordon, a jazz giant and one of the greats to emerge from LA's historic Central Avenue scene, remains the only professional musician nominated for an Academy Award for Best Actor.

With a classic clear sound and a legendary ability to improvise, Gordon started as a student of music teacher Samuel Browne at South LA's Jefferson High, but dropped out of high school in his senior year to join the Lionel Hampton

Orchestra. Gordon led a colorful and eventful, and sometimes tragic life and his life story (and musician Bud Powell's) inspired the French director Bertrand Tavernier to tell a portion of it in the 1986 film drama "Round Midnight," and cast him in a lead role. His father, Dr. Frank Gordon, was one of the first African American doctors in LA. Born and raised in South LA, Gordon used music as a vehicle to travel the world.

ETTA JAMES

THE GREATEST BLUES SINGER OF MODERN TIMES

(b. 1938 – d. 2012)

An amazingly powerful vocalist and talented songwriter, Etta James—the greatest blues singer of modern times—started singing lessons at the tender age of five. Few female Rhythm and Blues stars have enjoyed the consistent acclaim that James (nee Jamesetta Hawkins), received throughout a career that spanned six decades. In 1954, the grown-up Etta James initiated a string of hits that included the all-time classic songs "At Last", "I'd Rather Go Blind" and "Something's Got a Hold on Me".

Once forgotten by the music industry, in the 1990's through the early 2000's, James won six Grammy Awards, 17 Blues Music Awards, was inducted into the Rock and Roll Hall of Fame in 1993, the Grammy Hall of Fame in 1999 and the Blues Hall of Fame in 2001. Ranked number 22 on the list of the 100 Greatest

Singers of All Time; ranked number 62 on the list of the 100 Greatest Artists of All Time. James was born, raised and lived much of her life in South LA.

ELVIRA "VI" REDD

THE FIRST WOMAN JAZZ SAXOPHONIST TO PLAY WITH MAJOR JAZZ BANDS

(b. 1928)

Daughter of an influential Central Avenue jazz drummer and nightclub owner, Elvira Redd was the first woman jazz saxophone player in the 1940's and 50's to play with the major jazz bands of the day. In 1962, Redd released "Bird Call," her first album, and in 1963, she released her second titled "Lady Soul." During her career, Redd played with Count Basie, Dexter Gordon, Earl Hines, Dizzy Gillespie and Sara Vaughn and participated in tours of Britain, France, Japan, Spain, and Sweden. Redd received recognition from the Academy of Television Arts and Sciences in the documentary titled "Instrumental Women: Celebrating Women in Jazz."

In 1989 Redd received a Lifetime Achievement Award from the Los Angeles Jazz Society. In 2001, Redd received the Mary Lou Williams 'Women in Jazz Award'

from the Kennedy Center. Redd, a graduate of California State University, Los Angeles, earned a teaching certificate from USC. Redd was born, raised and continues to live in South LA.

FERDINAND JELLY ROLL MORTON

THE FIRST COMPOSER OF JAZZ MUSIC

(b. 1890 – d. 1941)

In 1915, Ferdinand Jelly Roll Morton's composition "Jelly Roll Blues" became one of the first jazz compositions published in the world, and the recordings of his band Jelly Roll Morton & His Red Hot Peppers are considered classics of 1920's jazz.

Considered by many to be the first published composer of jazz music, Morton, a ragtime pianist from New Orleans and bandleader, also wrote "King Porter Stomp," "Wolverine Blues," "Black Bottom Stomp," and "I Thought I Heard Buddy Bolden Say." Morton, a Rock and Roll Hall of Fame inductee, was born in New Orleans, first arrived in Southern California in 1916 and lived in South LA from 1917 until 1922, and returned on and off until his death in 1941 at LA County Hospital. In 2005, Jelly Roll Morton received a posthumous Lifetime Achievement Grammy from the Recording Industry Association of America.

GERALD WILSON

TRUMPETER, BIG BAND ORCHESTRAL LEADER AND CREATOR OF THE CALIFORNIA JAZZ SOUND

(b. 1918 – d. 2014)

Though he first established himself as part of South LA's Central Avenue jazz scene in the 1940's, acclaimed jazz master Gerald Wilson remains one of LA's better-kept musical secrets. In 1960, he formed an LA-based twenty-member recording band that made a series of critically acclaimed recordings for the Pacific Jazz label. The 1968 album California Soul is a classic. "Wilson was a member of the faculty at California State University, Los Angeles and the University of California, Los Angeles, for many years recently winning a "teacher of the year" award. In the 1970s he also served on the faculty at California State University, Northridge, where he taught Jazz History to wide acclaim among the student body, and has also taught at Cal Arts in Los Angeles."

In 1990, trumpeter, arranger, big band leader, composer, and educator Gerald Wilson was recognized as a Master of Jazz by the United States' National Endowment of Arts. In 1996, the Library of Congress Gerald Wilson created

an archive of his life's work. In 1997, Wilson received the American Jazz Award for Best Arranger and Best Big Band. In, 2008 he received the Monterey Jazz Festival Jazz Legends Award, and, in 2012 the Los Angeles County Museum of Art/Los Angeles Jazz Society L.A. Jazz Treasure Award. Born and raised in Mississippi, Wilson lived in South LA from the 1940's until his demise in 2014.

HADDA BROOKS

QUEEN OF THE BOOGIE AND THE FIRST AFRICAN AMERICAN WOMAN TO HOST A TV SHOW IN THE U.S.

(b. 1916 – d. 2002)

In 1957, Hadda Brooks became the first African American woman in the entire United States of America to host her own television show. The Hadda Brooks Show, a combination talk and musical entertainment show, aired on Los Angeles' KCOP. The show opened with Brooks seated behind a grand piano, cigarette smoke curling about her. She appeared in 26 half-hour episodes of the show.

Brooks—a world-class pianist, vocalist, and composer—sang at Hawaii's statehood ceremony in 1959 and was asked for a private audience by Pope Pius XII. Ms. Brooks lived a multifaceted celebrity life, singing to Humphrey Bogart in "In a Lonely Place," and marrying a Harlem Globetrotter. Ms. Brooks frequented the blues clubs on Central Avenue and met Billie Holiday in a bathroom when Holiday opened the door of Ms. Brooks' stall and offered her a hit on her marijuana cigarette."

Her first single, "Swinging the Boogie," which she composed, was issued in 1945. In the 1970's, she performed in nightclubs and festivals across Europe. In 1993, Ms.

Brooks was presented with the Prestigious Pioneer Award by Bonnie Raitt on behalf of the Smithsonian-based Rhythm and Blues Foundation." In 2007, a 72-minute movie documentary, "Hadda Brooks, Queen of the Boogie," directed by Austin Young and Barry Pett, was presented at the Los Angeles Silver Lake Film Festival and made into a feature-length film released in 2012. Brooks was born, raised, lived, and died in South LA.

HAMPTON HAWES

LEGENDARY JAZZ PIANIST AND MEMOIRIST

(b. 1928 – d. 1977)

Son of a minister and a church pianist, the highly regarded bebop pianist Hamilton 'Hampton' Hawes recorded nine albums, played sold-out shows and concert halls in ten countries, and was covered widely in the press, including appearances on European television and radio. Entirely self-taught, by the time he was 16 years old he was playing with some of the best jazz musicians on the West Coast. Hawes fell victim to drug addiction and was arrested in 1958. In 1963, he received a pardon from president John F. Kennedy.

Hawes memoir, Raise Up Off Me, an autobiography written with Don Asher was published in 1974, shedding light on his heroin addiction, the bebop movement, and his friendships with some of the leading jazz musicians of his time.

It was the first book about the bebop era written by a musician and won the ASCAP Deems Taylor Award for music writing in 1975. Critic Gary Giddins,

who wrote the book's introduction, called it a "major contribution to the literature of jazz." The Penguin Guide to Jazz cites it as "one of the most moving memoirs ever written by a musician, and a classic of jazz writing." In 2004, the Los Angeles City Council passed a resolution declaring November 13 "Hampton Hawes Day." Hampton Hawes was born, raised, lived, and died in South LA.

IVIE ANDERSON

DUKE ELLINGTON ORCHESTRA'S MOST FAMOUS FEMALE JAZZ SINGER

(b. 1905 — d. 1945)

A jazz singer best known for performing with the Duke Ellington Orchestra from 1931 to 1942, Andersen also appeared in two movies during 1937—"A Day at the Races," and "Hit Parade." Anderson's singing career began around 1921 with performances in Los Angeles. Jazz critic Nat Hentoff said Anderson is "easily the most sensitive and musical female vocalist Ellington ever had... She sang with a simplicity ... so artless that she is ... remarkably neglected in ... writings about jazz...She sang with a supple warmth and caressing beat that made her one of the unforgettable voices in Jazz...direct, completely unpretentious and ungimmicked."

In the 40's and 50's, she operated Ivie's Chicken Shack on Central and Vernon. Born in Gilroy, CA, Anderson grew up in what is now the "52nd Place Historic District", lived until the age of 45, and died in South LA.

LESTER YOUNG

JAZZ HIPSTER, MASTER OF THE TENOR SAXOPHONE, STYLE ICON AND POPULIZER OF "COOL"

(b. 1909 – d. 1959)

Nicknamed "Prez" by jazz great Billie Holiday, Lester Young is remembered as one of the finest and most influential tenor sax players on the jazz scene and arguably the coolest person of all time. Young's tailored suits, *"porkpie hat style", weed-smokin,' and way of talkin'* made him a fashion icon and a living jazz legend. He is said to have coined the term 'bread' for money and to have popularized the use of the term "cool" to mean ... well ... something "cool," and to have established, invented, or popularized most of the hipster slang associated with jazz music.

Upon his death "Charles Mingus dedicated an elegy to Young, "Goodbye Pork Pie Hat," only a few months after his death. Wayne Shorter, then of Art Blakey's Jazz Messengers, composed a tribute, called "Lester Left Town." In 1981, Charles F. Gordon published the book *The Resurrection of Lady Lester*, subtitled *A Poetic Mood Song Based on the Legend of Lester Young."* The work was subsequently adapted for the theater and was staged in November of that year at the Manhattan Theater Club, New York City, with a four-piece jazz combo led by Dwight Andrews.

In the 1986 film "Round Midnight," the fictional main character Dale Turner, played by Dexter Gordon, was partly based on Young—incorporating flashback-references of his army experiences, and loosely depicting his time in Paris and his return to New York—just before his death. Young is a major character in English writer Geoff Dyer's 1991 fictional book about jazz, But Beautiful. The 1994 documentary about the 1958 Esquire article called "A Great Day in Harlem" featured the photographs of jazz musicians, and the comments they made about Young. For many of the other participants, the photo shoot was the last time they saw him alive, he was the first musician in the famous photo to pass away.

Young, the oldest son in a large musical family from New Orleans that moved to South LA in 1929, played in the jazz clubs along South LA's Central Avenue during the 1940's and left to travel the world.

MELBA LISTON

PIONEERING JAZZ TROMBONIST AND EXQUISITE ARRANGER

(b. 1926 – d. 1999)

Though she was primarily known for her skills as a jazz arranger, Melba Doretta Liston was born to play the trombone. Beginning when she was just seven years old, Liston grew up and became a force on the west coast jazz scene. She toured with Billie Holiday, Dexter Gordon, and Dizzy Gillespie, and became the first woman to play with Gerald Wilson's Big Band. In the late 1940's, Liston returned to LA and worked as a clerk for the Los Angeles School District's Board of Education.

In 1948, Liston began a second career as an arranger at a time when being an arranger was dominated by men. Liston's career helped pave the way for women in jazz in roles other than as vocalists. Melba Liston is recognized as a pioneering woman in jazz and as a great jazz musician. Liston was featured in the 2013 documentary film about women jazz and big band instrumentalists titled "The Girls in the Band." Born in Kansas City, Missouri, Liston lived, made beautiful music, and died in South LA.

SOUTH LA'S LITERARY & JOURNALISTIC GIANTS

PUBLISHERS, POLITICIANS, POETS AND A LIBRARIAN

In Chapter Nine, we meet South LA's leaders of journalism and literature such as the following: the educator, author, and poet known as one of the leading literary figures of the Harlem Renaissance, Arnaud "Arna" Bontemps; the first African American woman newspaper publisher-editor in California, educator and civil rights activist, Charlotta Bass; the author of hard-boiled crime fiction novels and master of the noir genre, Chester Himes; the man who built a 13-newspaper publishing empire, Chester Washington; the first African American newspaper owner in California and mentor extraordinaire to Charlotta Bass, John J. Neimore; the founder and first publisher of the Los Angeles Sentinel, the largest Black-owned African American owned newspaper on the west coast, Leon Washington; the first African American librarian in California and the first to be hired by the LA public library system, Miriam Matthews; the national award-winning journalist and Hip-Hop Slam Poetry Champ of New York City, Paul Beatty; and, the writer referred to as the "LA Blueswoman" and the unofficial poet laureate of Los Angeles, Wanda Coleman.

ARNAUD "ARNA" BONTEMPS

LEADING LITERARY FIGURE OF THE HARLEM RENAISSANCE

(b. 1902 – d. 1973)

In 1903—at the age of three—future poet, novelist, librarian, and member of the Harlem Renaissance—Arna Bontemps moved to South LA as a child with his family. He grew up in California, attended the San Fernando Boarding Academy as a teen, and graduated from Pacific Union College in 1923. In 1924, Bontemps accepted a teaching position, moved to New York, became a part of the Harlem Renaissance, and the rest is history.

Bontemps' work includes several books of fiction, numerous short stories, and the 1945 novel "Anyplace But Here," in which he speaks about growing up in Watts. Through his librarianship and bibliographic work, Bontemps became a leading figure in establishing African American literature as a legitimate object of study and preservation. Bontemps' work as a poet, novelist, children's writer, editor, librarian, and historian helped shape modern African American literature, but it also had a tremendous influence on African American culture.

Bontemps received numerous awards and honors including the *Opportunity* magazine Alexander Pushkin Poetry Prize (1926, 1927), the Crisis poetry prize

(1927), Opportunity magazine short story prize (1932), Rosenwald Fellowships (1938, 1942), Guggenheim Fellowships (1949, 1954), Jane Addams Children's Book Award for *The Story of the Negro* (1948) (1956), James L. Dow award for *Anyplace But Here* (1967), and honorary doctorates in literature from Morgan State College (1969), and Berea College (1973). Born in Louisiana, Bontemps was raised in Watts and became an integral part of the black cultural renaissance of the 1920's.

CHARLOTTA BASS

CIVIL RIGHTS ACTIVIST, JOURNALIST, NEWSPAPER OWNER, AND FIRST AFRICAN AMERICAN WOMAN NOMINATED FOR VICE PRESIDENT OF UNITED STATES

(b. 1874 – d. 1969)

Multidimensional Charlotta Bass was a journalist, newspaper publisher-editor, community educator, civil rights activist, and politician, and leader of California's first African American newspaper, the *California Eagle*, from 1912 to 1951. In 1911, at the age of 36, Bass first landed in LA and went to work for John Neimore, founder of the *California Eagle* newspaper. Neimore mentored her in the workings of a black newspaper, emphasizing the importance of political activism, racial justice advocacy, and the urgent need to defend and expand the rights of African Americans.

Neimore suffered from poor health and, in 1912, on his deathbed, Neimore turned the *California Eagle* over to Bass who ran it for the next 40 years. At its height, the newspaper had a circulation of 60,000, making it the largest African American newspaper on the West Coast. Referring to the press, Bass said "African American newspapers are instrumental in fostering community consciousness."

As a civil rights activist, Bass fought against the Ku Klux Klan and racial bias. In 1950, Mrs. Bass attended the conferences in Prague, Czechoslovakia on the Defenders of the Peace Committee of the World CONGRESS. and subsequently visited the Soviet Union. Mrs. Bass was impressed with the Soviet Union's policies on racial issues. "I will never forget the moment when I first realized, standing there in the great Georgian University, that there is in very truth not even a semblance of racial exclusiveness in Russia."

Later in 1950, Bass joined the Progressive Party and ran for Congress. In 1952, she was selected to run for Vice-President on the Progressive Party ticket. In 1952, Charlotta Bass became the first African American woman selected to run for Vice President of the United States by the Progressive Party. Born in Rhode Island on Valentine's Day, Bass lived and died in South LA.

CHESTER HIMES

EXPATRIATE AUTHOR OF HARD-BOILED CRIME NOVELS AND MASTER OF THE NOIR GENRE

(b. 1909 – d. 1984)

Typically set in the 1950s and early 1960s, Himes works—some of which have been filmed—include the *Harlem Detective* series of novels for which he is best known, featuring two black policemen called *Grave Digger Jones* and *Coffin Ed Johnson*. In the early 1940's, while working as a screenwriter in Los Angeles, Himes wrote two novels about LA—*If He Hollers Let Him Go*, published in 1945, and The Lonely Crusade, published in 1947. Both books deal with the experience of the wave of black immigrants drawn to LA by the city's defense industries, and their experiences dealing with the established African American community, unions and management.

By the 1950's, having given up on making progress in the United States of America due to racism and discrimination, Himes decided to move to France permanently. In 1958, Himes won France's Grand Prix de Littérature Policière.

In his autobiography, Himes wrote: "Up to the age of thirty-one I had been hurt emotionally, spiritually and physically as much as thirty-one years can bear. I had lived in the South, I had fallen down an elevator shaft, I had been kicked out of college, I had served seven and a half years in prison, I had survived the humiliating last five years of Depression in Cleveland, and still I was entire, complete, functional, my mind was sharp, my reflexes were good, and I was not bitter.

But under the mental corrosion of race prejudice in Los Angeles, I became bitter and saturated with hate."

In 1972 Himes finished the first of two autobiographies *The Quality of Hurt: The Early Years; The Autobiography of Chester Himes* followed in 1976 by *My Life of Absurdity: The Later Years; The Autobiography of Chester Himes.*

Born in Louisiana, Himes lived, and published two novels, in South LA.

CHESTER WASHINGTON

BUILDER OF A 13-NEWSPAPER PUBLISHING EMPIRE

(b. 1902 – d. 1983)

In the 1920's, journalist, editor and future newspaper publisher Chester Washington started his newspaper career as a stenographer, journalist, and sports editor with the Pittsburgh, Pennsylvania's *Courier*. In 1955, Washington moved to LA and became the first African American news employee at the LA Mirror-News. In 1962, he went to work for the LA Sentinel, the city's largest Black-owned weekly, where he became editor-in-charge.

In 1966, Washington began building a 13-newspaper publishing empire called Central News-Wave Publications. Washington, through his 'Sez Ches' by Chester L. Washington series, used his editor position as a pulpit for civil rights.

In 1982, former LA County Supervisor Kenneth Hahn dedicated the Chester L. Washington Golf Course at 1818 Charlie Sifford Dr, LA 90047, one of the first public golf courses in LA to allow African Americans to play in his honor. Born in Pittsburg, Washington lived and died in South LA.

JOHN NEIMORE

FOUNDED THE THE CALIFORNIA EAGLE, THE FIRST AFRICAN AMERICAN NEWSPAPER IN THE WESTERN U.S.

(b. 1862 – d. 1912)

In the late 1800's, newspapers owned by white men either denigrated or ignored African Americans. In 1879, John Neimore established California's original African American publication The *California Owl*, to help newly arrived African Americans adapt to life in Los Angeles. Later, in 1895, he established The *California Eagle* which, until its demise, was the oldest African- American newspaper on the west coast. The *Eagle's* goal was to provide helpful information and inspiration to LA's growing African American community.

Neimore, a founding member of the Second Baptist Church in South Central LA, used his influence to highlight issues faced by African Americans in our daily lives, including race relations and politics. In 1912, Neimore was in very

poor health and, on his deathbed, turned control of the paper over to his dynamic mentee Charlotta Bass, making her the first African American woman to own a newspaper. Bass ran the California Eagle until she retired in 1951. Born in Texas, Neimore moved to LA as a teenager and lived, and died in South LA.

LEON H. WASHINGTON

FOUNDER OF THE LOS ANGELES SENTINEL, AMERICA'S SECOND LARGEST AFRICAN AMERICAN NEWSPAPER

(b. 1907 — d. 1974)

In 1933, after working for years at the *California Eagle*, California's most prominent African American newspaper, civil rights activist Leon H. Washington founded the Eastside Shopper and promptly renamed it *The Los Angeles Sentinel*. Washington's *Sentinel* soon became a competitive rival to the Eagle. Washington used the *Sentinel* to champion economic equality and entrepreneurship for its mostly African American readership.

One of several publishers in the African American community who used their newspapers as platforms to fight racial discrimination, Washington is best known for taking on the Central Avenue merchants with his "Don't Spend Where You Can't Work" campaign.

In 1949, Washington called for a series of non-violent demonstrations against white merchants who operated in the African American community, but who refused to hire black workers. Because he was jailed in one of the demonstra-

tions, he subsequently became more widely admired in the local black community. The city of LA honored Washington's contribution to civic life by dedicating Colonel Leon H. Washington Park at 8908 Maie Ave, LA 90002 in his name. Born in Kansas, Washington moved to LA in 1933 and lived, worked, owned property, and fought discrimination through journalism in South LA.

MIRIAM MATTHEWS

FIRST AFRICAN AMERICAN LIBRARIAN LICENSED IN CALIFORNIA AND FIRST HIRED IN THE LA PUBLIC LIBRARY SYSTEM

(b. 1905 – d. 2003)

After spending two years at UCLA, graduating from UC Berkeley in 1926 and earning a certificate in librarianship, Miriam Matthews, in 1927, became the first credentialed African- American librarian in California, and the first Black librarian hired by the LA Public Library system. While working within the library system, the history-minded Matthews identified "a small collection of books on the Negro" and began building that into a substantial research collection documenting the contributions made by African Americans to California's history and culture.

In the 1940s, Matthews—initially as a member, and later as Chair of the Committee on Intellectual Freedom—participated in a successful effort to prevent the establishment of a board of censors in the Los Angeles County

Public Library. As part of her commitment to honor African American contributions, Matthews pioneered efforts to establish a "Negro History Week" (now Black History Month) in Los Angeles in 1929, and she remained involved in the annual celebration thereafter.

Her essay for the California African American Museum was used in support of efforts to rename a Manhattan Beach neighborhood Bruce's Beach, in honor of the African American family that established a resort called Bruce's Lodge in that location in 1912. In 1981, she was appointed to the Los Angeles Bicentennial Committee's History Team. She helped to document the city's multiracial origins, which resulted in a monument at El Pueblo de Los Angeles State Historic Park listing all of the city's founders (los pobladores) by name, race, sex, and age (26 Blacks, 16 Native Americans, and two Whites).

The Miriam Matthews Branch Library on Florence Ave in Hyde Park is named in her honor. Born in Florida, Matthews, who moved to South LA at two years old with her family, was raised, educated, and lived in South LA. The Miriam Matthews Photograph Collection consists of 4,600 black and white photographs of varying sizes, negatives, captions, and descriptions from museum exhibitions, and a slide carousel. The collection reflects Matthews' dedication to the preservation of African American history in Los Angeles.

PAUL BEATTY

AWARD-WINNING JOURNALIST AND GRAND HIP-HOP POETRY SLAM CHAMPION

(b. 1962)

In 1990, award-winning poet, author, editor, and associate professor of writing at Columbia University Paul Beatty, was crowned the first-ever Grand Poetry Slam Champion of the Nuyorican Poets café, resulting in his first volume of poetry, *Big Bank Take Little Bank*. In 1993, he used a grant from the Foundation for Contemporary Arts Grants to produce his first novel, *The White Boy Shuffle* in 1996, and his second *Tuff* in 2000.

In 2016, he won the National Book Critics Circle Award and the Mann Booker Prize for his novel *The Sellout*, the first time a writer from the United States was honored with the Mann Booker. In 2017, the International Dublin Literary Award also honored *The Sellout*. The book, a rumbustious, lyrically poetic novel was turned down, by no fewer than 18 publishers. Beatty, who received an M.A. in Psychology from Boston University, and an M.F.A. in Creative Writing from Brooklyn College, was born and raised in South LA.

WALTER MOSLEY

GRAND MASTER OF MYSTERY WRITERS, BEST-SELLING AUTHOR, AND FATHER OF THE "EASY RAWLINS" SERIES

(b. 1952)

Perhaps best known for the crime mysteries featuring Ezekiel "Easy" Porterhouse Rawlins, the hard-boiled Black private investigator living from Watts, Mosley ranks among the most acclaimed crime novelists of our time. Author of more than sixty books, Mosley's books have been translated into more than twenty-five languages.

Mosley's body of work also includes other fictional crime mysteries, graphic novels such as *Maximum Fantastic Four*, written with Stan Lee of Marvel Comics in 2005, non-fiction books, plays, and science fiction.

Mosley has won numerous literary awards including the Edgar Award for *Down the River Unto the Sea*, the O. Henry Award, induction into the New York State Writers Hall of Fame, the 2016 Mystery Writers of America's Grand

Master Award, a Grammy, several NAACP Image awards, PEN America's Lifetime Achievement Award, the LA Times Festival of Books Robert Kirsch Award for Lifetime Achievement, and the National Book Foundation's 2020 Medal for Distinguished Contribution to American Letters.

WANDA COLEMAN

THE LA BLUESWOMAN AND UNOFFICIAL POET LAUREATE OF LOS ANGELES

(b. 1946 – d. 2013)

Known as "the LA Blueswoman" poet and writer, Wanda Coleman won critical acclaim for her unusually prescient and often innovative work but struggled to make a living from her craft. The author of 20 books of poetry and prose, Coleman's work is focused on racism and the outcast status of living below the poverty line in her long-time home, Los Angeles. Her subjects are often controversial and her tone unapologetic.

"Coleman frequently writes to illuminate the lives of the underclass and the disenfranchised, the invisible men and women who populate America's downtown streets after dark, the asylums and waystations, the inner-city hospitals and clinics," Tony Magistrale wrote *in Black American Literature Forum*. "Wanda Coleman, like Gwendolyn Brooks before her, has much to tell us about what it is like to be a poor black woman in America."

Coleman's poetry, full of creative vigor, often dealt with racism and violence, poverty and love, family, and Los Angeles. The Watts-born Coleman began taking writing workshops after the 1965 Watts riots, when she was already a wife and mother. Her first collection of poetry, the *Art in the Court of the Blue Fag*, was published in 1977 by West Coast independent publisher Black Sparrow Press. Coleman found a home at Black Sparrow, known for publishing famed poet Charles Bukowski. Black Sparrow published her collections *Mad Dog Black Lady*, *Imagoes*, *Hand Dance* and *Bathwater Wine*, among others.

In all, Coleman published more than 20 books of poetry, essays, and short fiction. Coleman said: "Words seem inadequate in expressing the anger and outrage I feel at the persistent racism that permeates every aspect of black American life. Since words are what I am best at, I concern myself with this as an urban actuality as best I can."

The city has been a vital part of her writings and an important outlet for her poetry readings. Coleman, said poet Juan Felipe Herrera, was the "word-caster of live coals of Watts & LA" In November of 2015, the Ascot branch of the Los Angeles Public Library in Watts, where Coleman spent many of her formative years reading and writing, was renamed the Wanda Coleman Branch Library by the City of LA in her honor. Wanda Coleman was born and raised in the Watts neighborhood of South LA.

SOUTH LA'S JURISPRUDENCE DREAM TEAM

LAWYERS, DISTRICT ATTORNEY'S, JUDGES, AND A LEGAL PROFESSOR

In Chapter Ten, we meet members of South LA's legal dream team like the first African American to graduate from the UCLA School of Law, and one of the first three African Americans elected to LA City Council, Billy G. Mills; the practicing dentist who went to night school to become the first African American graduate of Loyola Law School and a NAACP fighter for civil rights, Dr. H. Claude Hudson; the first woman and the first African American to serve as LA County's District Attorney, USC Law School graduate, Jackie Lacey; the first male African American to serve in the role of Assistant District Attorney for LA County and lead lawyer on OJ's Dream Team, the "if it don't fit, you must acquit" superlawyer, Johnnie Cochran; the first African American graduate of Stanford Law School, professor emeritus of law, former chief counsel for the United States Department of Transportation, Sallyanne Payton; and the first African American lawyer admitted to the Los Angeles Bar Association, and the first black to be elected to the California Municipal Court, Thomas Griffith Jr.

BILLY G. MILLS

FIRST AFRICAN AMERICAN TO RECEIVE JURIS DOCTORATE AT UCLA AND ONE OF THE FIRST THREE AFRICAN AMERICANS ELECTED TO LA CITY COUNCIL

(b. 1929)

After receiving an Associate in Arts from Compton College in 1951, Billy G. Mills earned Bachelor of Arts degrees in English and Political Science from UCLA. In 1954, Mills, a member of the first graduating class to complete the university's full three-year program, earned a law degree from UCLA and became the first African American student to receive the Juris Doctorate degree from UCLA.

In 1963, along with Gilbert Lindsay and the future four-term Mayor of LA, Tom Bradley, Mills became one of the first three African Americans elected to the Los Angeles City Council. Mills served on the council until April 3, 1974, when—then-California Governor and future-President Ronald Reagan—appointed him to the California Superior Court bench. Mills, a supervising judge of family law for the Superior Court of Los Angeles, retired from judicial service in 1990.

In 1984, Mills was honored as "Alumnus of the Year" by the Board of directors of the UCLA Law Alumni Association. Born in Waco, Texas, Mills served and continues to live in South LA.

H. CLAUDE HUDSON

NAACP LAWYER, CIVIL RIGHTS ADVOCATE AND FIRST AFRICAN AMERICAN GRADUATE OF LOYOLA LAW SCHOOL

(b. 1887 — d. 1989)

In 1913, H. Claude Hudson earned a degree in dentistry from historically black Howard University. Hudson and his family moved to Los Angeles in 1923 where he practiced dentistry and served as the president of the Los Angeles Chapter of the NAACP. Later, in 1931, while working as a dentist during the daytime, Hudson became the first African American graduate of Loyola Law School in LA.

He went to work for the NAACP to fight for justice and against inequality. Perhaps best-known as a civil rights advocate and bank founder, Hudson was instrumental in desegregating Los Angeles County beaches and establishing Martin Luther King Jr Hospital in Watts. Later, as a promi-nent businessman and advocate for civil rights, Hudson helped found the

Broadway Federal Savings and Loan Association, the nation's second-larg-est African American-owned saving and loan. The H. Claude Hudson Comprehensive Health Center in historic south central Los Angeles at 829 S Grand Ave, LA 90007 is named in his honor. Born in Louisiana, moving to LA as a young adult, and contributing to the city, Hudson died in South LA.

JACKIE LACEY

FIRST WOMAN AND FIRST AFRICAN AMERICAN LA COUNTY DISTRICT ATTORNEY

(b. 1957)

In winning the 2012 election, Jackie Lacey became the first woman and the first African American District Attorney of LA County. Lacey grew up in the Crenshaw district, attended Dorsey High School, earned a bachelor's degree from the University of California, Irvine in 1979, and a J.D. from the University of Southern California Gould School of Law in 1982. Lacey served over thirty

years as a courtroom prosecutor in the DA's office and, in 2012, was elected LA County's first African American and first woman DA. Lacey was born and raised in the Crenshaw District of South LA.

JOHNNIE COCHRAN

FIRST AFRICAN AMERICAN MALE ASSISTANT DISTRICT ATTORNEY IN LA COUNTY AND LEAD DEFENSE LAWYER FOR OJ SIMPSON

(b. 1937 – d. 2005)

In 1978, Johnnie Cochran, one of our greatest lawyers of the 20th Century, became the first African American male to serve as the assistant district attorney for Los Angeles County, California.

Prior to becoming the lead defense lawyer for O.J. Simpson's defense team in the Trial of the Century, Cochran was best known for police brutality and civil rights cases. Despite the strong case against Simpson, Cochran was able to convince the jury that there was reasonable doubt concerning the validity of the state's DNA evidence. Cochran and the defense team also alleged misconduct by the LAPD related to systemic racism and incompetence—actions and comments of Detective Mark Fuhrman, among them.

Cochran's classic line, "If it don't fit, you must acquit" was deeply rooted in African oral traditions, and it became the most famous legal utterance of the 20th century. The O.J. trial became historically significant because of the two very different reactions to the verdict, a divergence that the media dubbed the "racial gap." In 1996, Cochran described his involvement in the case in his book *Journey to Justice*.

Cochran graduated first in his class from LA High School in 1955. He earned a B.A. in business economics from UCLA in 1959, and a JD from the Loyola Law School in 1962. In 2006, the Los Angeles Unified School District renamed Mount Vernon Middle School—Cochran's boyhood middle school—to Johnnie L Cochran Jr. Middle School in his honor. Cochran also appeared in a few film and television shows. Born in Louisiana, Cochran was raised, lived, and died in South LA.

SALLYANNE PAYTON

FIRST AFRICAN AMERICAN GRADUATE OF STANFORD LAW SCHOOL AND FIRST AFRICAN- AMERICAN WOMAN APPOINTED TO UNIVERSITY OF MICHIGAN LAW SCHOOL FACULTY

(b. Unknown)

In 1968—at a time when there were very few African American women in the legal profession—Sallyanne Peyton became the first African American editor of the *Stanford Law Review*, and the first black graduate of Stanford's School of Law. Later, in 1976, she became the first African American woman to join the University of Michigan Law School faculty. Peyton's distinguished legal career includes service as chief counsel for the US Department of Transportation's Urban Mass Transportation Administration Program and professor emeritus at the University of Michigan Law School.

Payton describes herself as the product of LA's black middle class—with family, church, and school forming the patterns of her life. Her father was an insurance underwriter for Golden State Mutual, a black-owned LA company. Her mother was a school teacher at Dorsey High, which Payton herself attended. "When I was growing up, all of my mother's friends had master's degrees, many from USC.," Payton says. "They had careers in educa-

tion and government. That was the normal career path for educated black women." A graduate of Dorsey High, Payton was born and raised in South LA.

THOMAS GRIFFITH JR

FIRST AFRICAN AMERICAN ADMITTED TO THE LA BAR ASSOCIATION, FIRST AFRICAN AMERICAN ELECTED TO THE CALIFORNIA MUNICIPAL COURT AND FIRST AFRICAN AMERICAN ELECTED TO THE LA COUNTY SUPERIOR COURT

(b. 1902 – d. 1986)

Pioneering lawyer Thomas Griffith Jr, the son of Thomas Griffith Sr, the senior minister of South LA's influential Second Baptist Church, in 1931 became the first African American lawyer admitted to the Los Angeles Bar Association. From 1935 to 1950, Griffith Jr was a controversial president of the LA NAACP. Some members of the NAACP began to grumble about Griffith's refusal to delegate authority. A representative of the national NAACP sent to investigate concurred with this assessment. Griffith began to be further seen as inactive and out of step with his constituency.

On a key murder investigation that the community wanted investigated, Griffith sided with the mayor and provided him with political cover rather than risk his position by pushing for a fuller investigation. Despite dwindling membership during his tenure, the organization won lawsuits that: enabled African Americans and Mexican Americans to swim in Pasadena city pool, win an employment discrimination case against the City of Los Angeles, and win a California Supreme Court decision that invalidated real estate covenants.

In 1953, he was appointed to the position of judge on the Los Angeles Municipal Court by then- Governor Earl Warren. In 1960, he became the first African American elected to the LA Municipal Court. In 1961, he was elected presiding judge of the Municipal Court, the first African American elected in a Los Angeles countywide vote. Then, in 1968, he was elected to Superior Court, the first African American judge chosen by county voters. Born in Iowa, Griffith Jr was raised, lived, and served in South LA.

SOUTH LA'S MYTHOLOGICAL HEROES

THE SPIRIT OF CALIFORNIA, AN AFRO BLACK BELT, A BADASS BLACK DETECTIVE AND A JUNKMAN AND HIS SON

In Chapter Eleven, we meet South LA's fictitious, badass mythological figures like the crime fighting martial arts expert and soul brother from Watts, Black Belt Jones; the griffin-controlling, gold-holding, beautiful black African goddess, the Spirit of California, regal Queen Calafia; the hard-boiled African American Private Investigator from Watts, Ezekiel "Easy" Porterhouse Rawlins; and the hilarious Junkmen from South Central, Fred Sanford and his son Lamont.

BLACK BELT JONES

KUNG FU KICKIN' CRIME FIGHTER FROM WATTS

The mob crosses the wrong man when it takes on Black Belt Jones, a fictional martial arts teacher from Watts dedicated to uplifting young people through martial arts and taking on "The Man." In the 1974 classic blaxploitation martial arts movie directed by Robert Clouse and starring Jim Kelly and Gloria Hendry, Black Belt Jones and Sydney take on smack-running gangsters set on destroying the African American community.

In the film, when the Mafia learn plans for the construction of a new civic center, the gangsters buy up all the land at the intended building site except for a karate dojo owned by Pop Byrd (Scatman Crothers), who refuses to give up his property. Black Belt Jones (Jim Kelly), an expert martial artist

and hand-for-hire, is contacted by his old friend Pop to help protect the dojo. Pop's daughter Sydney (Gloria Hendry) returns home upon hearing of her father's sudden death. Jones and Sydney, with support from the police department, rob the Mafia, subdue the criminals, rid the community of smack (heroin) and save the Pop's dojo.

CALAFIA

THE AFRICAN QUEEN AND SPIRIT OF CALIFORNIA

The beautiful black queen, the Spirit of California, Califia was first introduced by 16th-century poet Garci Rodríguez de Montalvo in his epic novel Las Sergas de Esplandián (The Adventures of Esplandián). In the book, Califia is strikingly gorgeous, courageous, strong of limb, and large of person. Adorned with lavish jewelry and a crown of feathers and jewels, Califia wore a robe decorated with images of the animals that roamed through her domain.

Full in the bloom of womanhood, Califia was the most beautiful of a long line of queens who ruled over the mythical island realm of California. Desirous

of achieving great things, Califia wanted to see the world and plunder a portion of it with an army of superior women warriors. Califia commanded a fleet of ships with which she used to go to surrounding lands to collect tribute. She also had an aerial defense force of griffins, fabulous flying animals trained to kill any man they found. A mural of Queen Califia can be found in the Mark Hopkins Hotel in San Francisco.

EZEKIEL "EASY" PORTERHOUSE RAWLINS

AFRICAN AMERICAN PRIVATE INVESTIGATOR FROM WATTS

Ezekiel "Easy" Rawlins is a fictional character created by mystery author Walter Mosley. Easy is an African American Private Investigator and World War II veteran living in the Watts neighborhood of Los Angeles. After first appearing in 1990, Easy has been featured in 14 novels and a 1995 film based on the novel "Devil in a Blue Dress".

As a private eye, Easy is always willing to do whatever it takes to get things done. He is featured in a series of best-selling mysteries set from the 1940s to the 1960s. The mysteries combine descriptions of racial inequities and

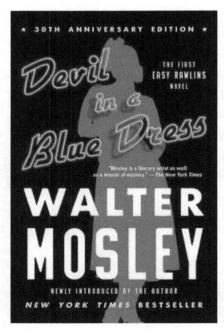

social injustice experienced by African Americans in Los Angeles. Easy's mother died when he was eight years old, and soon afterward his father fled to escape getting lynched after fighting with a white man. After growing up, Easy enlisted in the Army, settled in LA after the war where he purchased his first home and worked at an aircraft assembly plant. After getting in a dispute with his supervisor, he was fired leading him to take up his first case as an amatuer private investigator. Easy Rawlins was born on November 3, 1920, in New Iberia, Louisiana and lived in Watts, South LA.

FRED G. SANFORD AND LAMONT

HILARIOUS FATHER AND SON JUNKMEN FROM SOUTH CENTRAL

The fictional character Fred G. Sanford, played by comedian Redd Foxx on the TV shows Sanford and Son (1972-77), and Sanford (1980-81), is an elderly, widowed, father and a sarcastic, cantankerous and hilariously funny junk dealer from South Central LA. Fred, along with his son Lamont (played by actor Demond Wilson), runs Sanford and Son, a junk and antique dealership, out of their home. As the story goes, in 1946, Fred, his wife Elizabeth, and their son Lamont moved to the Watts neighborhood of Los Angeles. Fred was left with the responsibility of rearing Lamont alone after Elizabeth suddenly died several years later. Lamont dropped out of high school, subsequently joining his father in the junk business.

One of the main characteristics of Fred G. Sanford was that he had a weak heart and that he always knew that the day for 'The Big One' would eventually come. It was a trademark of the show that he would fake a heart attack in the face of some shocking news. Fred's catchphrase was, "You hear that, Elizabeth? I'm coming to join ya, honey!"

Fred G. Sanford was born in St. Louis, Missouri on January 20, 1907 (the episode "Happy Birthday, Pop" celebrated his 65th birthday that aired in 1972). In 1999 TV Guide ranked Fred G. Sanford #36 on its list of the 50 Greatest TV Characters of All Time.

SOUTH LA'S MOST SUCCESSFUL POLITICIANS

COUNCIL MEMBERS, MAYORS, A SUPERVISOR, STATE ASSEMBLYMEMBERS AND SENATORS, AND REPRESENTATIVES IN CONGRESS

In Chapter Twelve, we meet South LA's most successful politicians: the first female and first African American to serve as Mayor of Fontana, CA, Aquanetta Warren; the first African American elected to Congress from west of the Mississippi, Augustus Freeman Hawkins; former LAUSD Board Member, congressperson and ambassador to Micronesia, Diane Watson; the first Afro-Latino Mayor of LA, Francisco Reyes; newspaper owner and editor and the first African American elected to the California State Assembly, Frederick Madison Roberts; the first African American appointed to the LA City Council, and the self-proclaimed "Emperor of the Great 9th District," Gilbert Lindsay; public health leader, former speaker of the California House of Representatives, Congressperson Karen Bass; the only person to serve in the California State Assembly and Senate, on the LA County Board of Supervisors and on the LA City Council twice, accomplished politician, Mark Ridley-Thomas; former California state senator, current chairwoman of the U.S. House of Representatives financial services committee, Maxine Waters; former UCLA valedictorian and the first African American Nobel Peace Prize laureate, professor emeritus, Ralph Bunche; former member of the LA Unified School District board member, the first African American woman elected to LA City Council, Rita Walters; the former UCLA track athlete and LAPD cop, LA's first African American mayor, the only four-term mayor in the history of Los Angeles, Tom Bradley; and, the first African American woman from the West Coast elected to the U.S. Congress and the first member of congress to give birth while in office, Yvonne Brathwaite Burke.

AQUANETTA WARREN

FIRST WOMAN AND FIRST AFRICAN AMERICAN MAYOR OF FONTANA, CA

(b. Unknown)

Aquanetta Warren, the first female and first African American mayor of Fontana, was originally appointed to the Fontana City Council in 2002, served six years, and was re-elected twice. Warren was sworn in as Fontana's first female and first African American mayor in December of 2010 and was re-elected in 2014.

While in office, Mayor Warren held education summits with local schools, the community college district, and business leaders to outline plans preparing

the youth for future job markets. She also created the Healthy Fontana Program. In 2015, Warren was awarded the prestigious Health Champion Award from the California Center for Public Health. Born in Compton and raised in Watts, Warren resides in the Inland Empire.

AUGUSTUS FREEMAN HAWKINS

FIRST AFRICAN AMERICAN FROM CALIFORNIA ELECTED TO UNITED STATES HOUSE OF REPRESENTATIVES

(b. 1907 – d. 2007)

In 1935, Augustus F. Hawkins started his political career by winning an election to the California Assembly, where he served for 28 years. While in the state assembly seat, Hawkins guided countless pieces of legislation aimed at improving the lives of minorities and the urban poor including a fair housing act, a fair employment act, and workers compensation provisions for domestic workers.

By winning a Congressional seat in1963, Hawkins became the first African American from California, and the first from west of the Mississippi, to be elected to the United States House of Representatives. While there, Hawkins authored more than 300 state and federal laws, the most notable of which are Title VII of the Civil Rights Act of 1964 and the 1978 Humphrey-Hawkins Full Employment Act. Known by his colleagues on the Congressional BlackCaucus (CBC) as the "Silent Warrior," the longtime representative earned the respect of black leaders because he was determined to tackle social issues such as unemployment, and his commitment to securing equal educational opportunities for impoverished Americans.

Hawkins' political career of 56 years includes 28 years of public service in the California Assembly and 28 years in the United States Congress. The Augustus F. Hawkins Nature Park & Wetlands Nature Museum, located at 5790 Compton Ave, LA 90011, is named in his honor. Born in Louisiana, Hawkins was raised, lived, and died in South LA.

DIANE WATSON

HIGHLY EDUCATED WORLD TRAVELER AND ACCLAIMED LOCAL, STATEWIDE AND NATIONAL POLITICIAN

(b. 1933)

After graduating from Dorsey high School in South Los Angeles, future U.S. Congresswoman Diane Watson, received her Associate of Arts degree from Los Angeles City College in 1954 and a B.A. in Education from the University of California, Los Angeles UCLA in 1956. Later, Watson earned a Master's degree in School Psychology from California State University in 1967, and a Ph.D. in education administration from Claremont College in 1986.

Initially Interested in pursuing a career in education, Watson worked as a teacher and school psychologist in Los Angeles public schools, taught abroad in France and Japan, lectured at California State University (Long Beach and Los Angeles branches), and worked in the California Department of Education. Watson's political career began when she was elected to the Los Angeles Unified School Board in 1975. She served on the LAUSD School Board from 1975–78.

Subsequently, Watson was elected to the California State Senate and served from 1978 to 1998. Later, she served as the US Representative for California's 33rd Congressional District (i.e. Baldwin Hills and Ladera Heights) from 2003 until 2011. President Bill Clinton appointed her to serve as the U.S. States ambassador to Micronesia in 1999.

The Diane Watson Career Training Center, located at 3833 Crenshaw Blvd, LA 90008, is named in her honor. A graduate of Dorsey High and UCLA, Watson was born, raised, and continues to reside in South LA.

FREDERICK MADISON ROBERTS

FIRST AFRICAN AMERICAN GRADUATE OF LA HIGH, JOURNALIST, NEWSPAPER OWNER, AND FIRST AFRICAN AMERICAN ELECTED TO THE CALIFORNIA STATE ASSEMBLY

(b. 1879 – d. 1952)

In 1918, when LA's population was not quite 3% black, journalist, newspaper owner, editor, and the great-grandson of Sally Hemmings—consort of the slave-owning President Thomas Jefferson—Frederick Madison Roberts simultaneously became the first African American elected to the California State Assembly, and the first Black to hold statewide office on the Pacific coast.

Roberts represented the 62nd District, including Watts, which at the time was 70% white. In June 1922, Roberts welcomed Black nationalist leader Marcus Garvey of the UNIA to Los Angeles and rode in his parade car. Before being elected to the California Assembly, Roberts, the son of the owner of LA's first African American mortuary, was a successful mortician, newspaperman, and the co-founder of the LA Forum, one of the most important black organizations in LA during the early 1900's.

After being elected, Roberts served in the state assembly for 16 years, representing the district until 1934. During that period, he sponsored legislation that resulted in the establishment of UCLA, and improvements in public education. He also proposed several civil rights and anti-lynching measures.

Roberts also played an important role in civic religious affairs. He acted as a director for local branches of the National Association for the Advancement of Colored People, the YMCA, the Urban League, the Women's Political Study Club, and the Outdoor Health Association (i.e. see Dr. Leonard Stovall). In 1957 the city of Los Angeles dedicated Frederick M. Roberts Park on 4700 Honduras St in South LA, in his memory. On February 25, 2002, the California State Senate honored Frederick Madison Roberts for his contributions and service to the State of California. Roberts was born in Ohio, arrived in California at age six and lived, served. and died in South LA.

FRANCISCO REYES

FIRST AFRO-LATINO MAYOR (ALCALDE) OF LOS ANGELES

(b. 1749 – d. 1809)

In 1790, Francisco Reyes, the son of an Afro-Latino father and an Indigenous/Spanish mother, became both the first Afro-Latino alcalde (mayor) of the pueblo known as Los Angeles. Reyes, whose full name was Juan Francisco Reyes, was a Soldado de Cuero ("Leather-Jacketed Soldier") on the 1769 Portola expedition. He served as alcalde (of the Pueblo de Los Angeles for three terms—until 1795. Reyes was also the Spanish Crown's first land grantee and the original grantee of the San Fernando Rancho—now the San Fernando Valley.

By any measure of his times, he was a wealthy man. He later received a Spanish land grant for Rancho Los Encinos in the San Fernando Valley, and

subsequently received another in the Lompoc region. Reyes' lands included an area where the Catholic Church wanted to build a mission. Reyes sold the property to the church during his last year as mayor, and two years later—in 1797—the San Fernando Mission was completed. The Reyes family's historic home is now known as the Reyes Adobe Historical Site and is located in Agoura Hills California. Born in Baja California, Reyes lived and died in the Pueblo of Los Angeles.

GILBERT LINDSAY

FIRST AFRICAN AMERICAN ON THE LOS ANGELES CITY COUNCIL

(b. 1900 – d. 1990)

Lindsay came to Los Angeles from the Mississippi cotton fields in the late 1920s and started working for the Department of Water and Power. "I used to scrub toilets for the City of Los Angeles with a mop—that was my job," he once said. "I had so many toilets to clean every night. I was lower than a janitor—I had the lowest job you can give a human being."

From there, he took the Civil Service exam and became a clerk. He sat in a basement office by himself because his superiors did not want him to sit with whites. He became involved in grass-roots Democratic and labor politics. He became so entrenched that his DWP superiors called on him to help turn out the black vote on various bond issues. As the 1940s and '50s approached, Lindsay "was the man to see," recalled former Councilman Dave Cunningham.' (LA Times Obit. 12/29/90).

After his appointment to a vacant 9th District Council seat, Gilbert Lindsay, at the age of 62, became LA's first African American city council member. Lindsay, the self-proclaimed "Emperor of the Great 9th District," was

reelected to eight successive terms, ultimately serving 27 years—from 1963 to 1990—playing a critical role in shaping downtown LA. Lindsay had a show-business background.

During the 1940's, Lindsay was the manager/owner of Bilbrew and Lindsay Productions, which produced the pioneering broadcasts of the "Bronze Hour" on KGFJ Radio.

The program's announcer was A.C. Bilbrew, a prominent figure in South LA's choral music circles. "Councilman Lindsay was a dynamic force in Los Angeles who opened the doors of political power to all residents with his appointment to the City Council in January of 1963," said Mayor Tom Bradley, who once served beside Lindsay on the council.

On Lindsay's death at the age of 90, the mayor ordered all flags on city property to be flown at half-staff. Lindsay has been honored by the establishment of the Gilbert Lindsay Plaza at 1201 Figueroa Drive, LA 90015, and the Gilbert Lindsay Park and Recreation Center, and the Gilbert Lindsay Skatepark both located at 429, East 42nd Place, LA 90011. Born in Mississippi, Lindsay lived and died in South LA.

KAREN BASS

FIRST AFRICAN AMERICAN WOMAN IN THE U.S. TO BE SPEAKER OF A STATE LEGISLATURE

(b. 1953)

In the early 1990s, before her political career, Bass convened a small group of community organizers—both African Americans and Latinos—and founded the Community Coalition, known locally as CoCo. CoCo's mission is to help transform the social and economic conditions in South Los Angeles that foster addiction, crime, violence, and poverty by building a community institution that involves thousands in creating, influencing, and changing public policy.

In 2004, Bass was elected to represent the 47th district in the California State Assembly. In 2008, she was elected to serve as the 67th Speaker of the California State Assembly, becoming the first African American woman in United States history to serve as a speaker of a state legislative body. Bass completed her term in the state assembly seat in 2010.

On November 28, 2018, Bass was elected chair of the Congressional Black Caucus (CBC) during the 116th Congress. She also serves as chair of the United States House Foreign Affairs Subcommittee on Africa, Global Health, Global Human Rights and International Organizations. She also serves on

House Judiciary Subcommittee on Crime, Terrorism and Homeland Security. In November of 2020 Bass was reelected to represent the 37th Congressional District for a sixth term and, in October of 2021, she announced her candidacy for Mayor of LA. Bass was born and raised in LA, schooled at Hamilton High, and continues to serve South LA.

MARK RIDLEY-THOMAS

FIRST LA POLITICIAN TO SERVE IN THE CALIFORNIA ASSEMBLY, THE CALIFORNIA SENATE, ON THE LA COUNTY BOARD OF SUPERVISORS AND ON THE LA CITY COUNCIL

(b. 1954)

Mark Ridley-Thomas (MRT) was elected to the LA City Council in 1991, less than a year before the LA Riots. In its aftermath, the people of South LA fought to prevent the reestablishment of nuisance businesses, especially liquor stores. MRT said "We are going to use every means at our disposal to rid our community of these god-awful places of business, the kind of business they do is not good for the community."

In 2020, MRT was re-elected to the LA City Council for a final term making him the first person in LA's history to serve in the California Assembly (from 2002 until 2006), the California Senate (from 2006 to 2008), on the LA

Board of Supervisors (from 2008 to 2020), and the LA City Council (from 1991 to 2002 and 2020 to 2024).

On September 16, 2021, LA County honored by MRT for his three decades of public service by dedicating the Avis and Mark Ridley-Thomas Wellness Center and with these words, "(MRT) has made an indelible mark on count-less issues that have impacted our region - from leading efforts to address the homelessness crisis and supporting the development of thousands of affordable housing units to investing in both the physical and intellectual infrastructure needed to elevate underserved communities."

On October 13, 2021, the United States Attorney for the Central District of California announced that a federal grand jury had indicted MRT for "a bribery scheme in which his son, disgraced former California Assembly Member, Sebastian Ridley-Thomas, received substantial benefits from the USC in exchange for MRT supporting county contracts and lucrative contract amendments with the university." The indictment details how MRT allegedly misused his power as a supervisor in 2017 and 2018 to steer county contracts to USC in return for university payments to his son.

Presumed innocent until proven guilty, politician Mark Ridley-Thomas graduated from South LA's Manual Arts High School, earned a B.A. in Social Relations, an M.A. in Religious Studies, served as the Executive Director of the Southern California chapter of the legendary Southern Christian Leadership Conference, and earned a Ph.D. in Social Ethics and Policy Analysis from the University of Southern California (USC). MRT was born, raised, educated, and continues to live in South LA.

MAXINE WATERS

FIRST WOMAN AND FIRST AFRICAN AMERICAN TO CHAIR THE US HOUSE OF REPRESENTATIVES FINANCIAL SERVICES COMMITTEE

(b. 1938)

Elected in November 2018 to her fifteenth term in the U.S. House of Representatives—representing the 43rd Congressional District of California—Congresswoman Maxine Waters started her public service career in 1966 as an assistant teacher with the Head Start program in Watts. In 1971, Waters enrolled at Los Angeles State College, now California State University- Los Angeles, where she received a B.A. in Sociology.

In 1976, Waters was elected to the California State Assembly and served 14 years until 1990. In 1991, Waters was first elected to Congress, from 1997 to 1999. She chaired the Congressional Black Caucus and, in 2020, she sits as the most senior of the twelve African American women in Congress.

Waters is the first woman and the first African American to chair the U.S. House of Representatives Financial Services Committee. Born in Missouri, the fifth of 13 children reared by a single mother, Waters moved to South LA in 1961 and has served South LA since the mid-1970's.

RALPH BUNCHE

FIRST AFRICAN AMERICAN AWARDED THE NOBEL PEACE PRIZE

(b. 1904 — d. 1971)

His intellectual brilliance appeared early. Ralph Bunche was the valedictorian of his graduating class at Jefferson High School in Los Angeles, where he had been a debater and all-around athlete who competed in football, basketball, baseball, and track. At the University of California at Los Angeles, he supported himself with an athletic scholarship, which paid for his collegiate expenses, and with a janitorial job, which paid for his expenses. He played varsity basketball on championship teams, was active in debate and campus journalism, and graduated in 1927, summa cum laude, valedictorian of his class, with a major in international relations.

Bunche, a scholar and diplomat significant for his work with the United Nations, chaired the Department of Political Science at Howard University. While teaching at Howard University, he received a doctorate from Harvard University. On September 17, 1948, Count Bernadotte was assassinated, and Bunche was named acting UN mediator on Palestine.

After eleven months of virtually ceaseless negotiating, Bunche obtained signatures on armistice agreements between Israel and the Arab States. Bunche returned home to a hero's welcome. New York gave him a ticker-tape parade up Broadway, and the City of Los Angeles declared a "Ralph Bunche Day." He was besieged with requests to lecture, was awarded the Spingarn Prize by the NAACP in 1949, was given over thirty honorary degrees in the next three years, and the Nobel Peace Prize for 1950.

In 1955, he was appointed the UN Undersecretary for special political Affairs. Bunche is honored by the schools named in his honor in the cities of Carson, Compton, and Los Angeles. The Ralph Bunche Peace & Heritage Center is located in his boyhood home at 1221 East 40th, LA 90011 is a designated National Historic Landmark and as Los Angeles Historic-Cultural Monument #159. Born in Detroit, Bunche was raised and schooled in South LA.

RITA WALTERS

FIRST AFRICAN AMERICAN WOMAN ELECTED TO LA CITY COUNCIL

(b. 1930 – d. 2020)

In 1990, Walters became the first African American woman elected to the LA City Council (1990 - 2001) and a former member of the LA Unified School District Board of Education (2001 - 2016). During the tumultuous battle over mandatory busing in Los Angeles public schools in the late 1970s and 1980s, Rita Walters served as the only black member of a school board whose majority opposed forced integration.

When her pro-busing side won in court, she expressed dismay over an integration plan that excluded the black children of Watts. "I find it very interesting that the lines around the black community correspond almost to the street to the lines of the curfew area during the Watts uprising," she said in a 1980 interview, referring to the five days of rioting in 1965. "It becomes another stigma, another burden, that black people are asked to bear."

Walters, a trailblazing African American leader who advocated fiercely for racial equality on the LA school board from 1979 through 1991, and then on the LA City Council in the 1990s, died of complications from Alzheimer's disease and an infection. She was 89. Walters was largely on the losing side of the city's bitter integration wars, but she never gave up on her belief that

 children of different backgrounds would benefit by going to school together.

Through decades of public service, she extended her commitment to fighting for black workers and other minorities to gain equal access to employment. Prior to these positions, Walters served on the Board of Library Commissioners for the Los Angeles Public Library. Born in Chicago, Walters earned an MBA from the UCLA Anderson School of Management and lived, served, and died in South LA.

TOM BRADLEY

FIRST AFRICAN AMERICAN AND FIRST FOUR-TERM MAYOR OF LA

(b. 1917 – d.1998)

The first and—thus far—the only African American mayor of Los Angeles, Tom Bradley's 20 years in office mark the longest tenure by any mayor in the city's history. After leaving UCLA in 1940, Bradley began his career as a police officer with the Los Angeles Police Department. Bradley recalled incidents such as "the downtown department store that refused him credit, although he was a police officer, and the restaurants that would not serve blacks."

He told a LA Times reporter: "When I came to the department, there were literally two assignments for black officers. You either worked at Newton Street Division, which has a predominantly black community, or you worked traffic downtown. You could not work with a white officer, and that continued until 1964."

In April 1963, Bradley was elected to the LA City Council. In 1973, Bradley was elected mayor of LA and with four-terms and 20 years, is the longest-serving mayor in LA history. Several schools and the Tom Bradley International Terminal at Los Angeles International Airport is named in his honor. Bradley was born, raised, lived, served, and died in South LA.

YVONNE BRATHWAITE BURKE

FIRST AFRICAN AMERICAN WOMAN FROM WEST COAST IN CONGRESS, FIRST MEMBER OF CONGRESS TO GIVE BIRTH WHILE IN OFFICE, AND FIRST WOMAN AND FIRST AFRICAN- AMERICAN LA COUNTY SUPERVISOR

(b. 1932)

In 1953, future Congresswoman and LA County Supervisor, Yvonne Brathwaite Burke, earned a BA from UCLA. In 1956, Burke received a Juris Doctor degree from the University of Southern California School of Law. From 1967 through 1972, Burke served in the California State Assembly.

In 1973, Burke became the first female and first African American woman to represent the West Coast in the U.S. Congress where she represented the 93rd Congressional District until 1979. While there, Burke became the first United States congressperson to give birth during her political term. Burke was elected to the LA County Board of Supervisors in 1992, and became the first female and first African American LA County supervisor. She served until 2008. While on the board, Burke where she served as the chair three times (1993–94, 1997–98, 2002–03). In 2012, then-President Barack Obama appointed Burke to a position on the board of directors of Amtrak. Honored by having her name on the Yvonne Brathwaite Burke Senior Center, Burke—a graduate of Manual Arts High—was born, and raised in South LA.

SOUTH LA'S VOICES OF BLACK AMERICA

ROCHESTER, THE MAGNIFICENT MONTAGUE & MADAME A.C. BILBREW

In Chapter Thirteen, we meet a few of LA's barrier-breaking stars of radio such as the co-owner of Bilbrew and Lindsay Productions, which produced the pioneering broadcasts of the "Bronze Hour" on KGFJ Radio, and the first African American radio music program host in LA Madame A.C. Bilbrew; actor/comedian and Jack Benny' show co-star, the first African American with a recurring role on a National Radio Program, Eddie "Rochester" Anderson; and the man who coined the rallying cry of the '65 Watts riots, KGFJ DJ Magnificent "Burn, baby! Burn!" Montague.

A.C. BILBREW

FIRST AFRICAN AMERICAN RADIO MUSIC PROGRAM HOST IN LA

(b. 1891 — d. 1972)

The community leader, poet, musician, composer, playwright, clubwoman, actress, and radio personality known as Madame A. C. Bilbrew was also a leading figure in LA's gospel and choral music scene, where she was the choir director for a number of prominent black churches. In 1923, Bilbrew became the first black soloist to sing on a Los Angeles radio program. In 1929, Madame Bilbrew produced the first African American chorus that was filmed in Hollywood for the first African American 'talking' picture "Hearts in Dixie."

In the early 1940s, she hosted LA's first African American radio music program,

The Gold Hour. In 1955, her choral composition, "The Death of Emmett Till," was performed by Scatman Crothers and the Ramparts and released as a single, with a percentage of the royalties benefiting the NAACP. In 1974, she was honored by having her name attached to the A.C. Bilbrew County Public Library in Willowbrook. Educated at USC, Bilbrew was born in Arkansas and raised, lived, served, and died in South LA.

EDDIE "ROCHESTER" ANDERSON

ACTOR, DANCER, COMEDIAN, AND FIRST AFRICAN AMERICAN WITH RECURRING ROLE ON A NATIONAL RADIO PROGRAM

(b. 1905 – d. 1977)

The son of a minstrel and a tightrope walker, Eddie 'Rochester Anderson—star of radio, film, and television—was born into show business. Anderson appeared in more than 60 movies including "Gone With the Wind" in 1939 and "Cabin in the Sky" in 1943. Anderson became the first African American to have a regular role on a nationwide radio program and was among the highest-paid performers of his time.

Best known for his portrayal of the character 'Rochester' on the Jack Benny Radio Show, singer, comedian, and dancer Eddie Anderson received his big break while starring nightly at Central Avenue's Apex Club. Anderson was among the highest-paid performers of the time and invested wisely, eventually becoming very wealthy. Anderson, elected honorary Mayor of South LA's Central Ave—a position he took somewhat seriously—also has a star on the Hollywood Walk of Fame for Radio, was inducted into the Radio Hall of Fame in 2001, and had Rochester Circle in West Adams named in his honor. Born in Oakland, Anderson lived, worked, and died in South LA.

MAGNIFICENT MONTAGUE

ROCKED THE MIC DURING THE WATTS RIOTS

(b. 1928)

Notable not only for the soul music records he helped promote on KGFJ Los Angeles, the Magnificent Montague's signature catchphrase, "Burn, baby! Burn!" became the rallying cry of the '65 Watts riots. When rioters in Watts, California, began shouting "Burn, Baby! BURN!" in the turmoil of 1965, they were echoing the most popular cry on rhythm-and-blues radio: The trademark of Magnificent Montague, the most exciting R&B disc jockey ever to stroll through Soulsville.

One of the all-time baddest LA DeeJays notable not only for the soul music he promoted on KGFJ, Montague's popular catch-phrase was referenced in the Apollo 11 software code that took America to the moon: "The Burn, Baby, Burn – Master Ignition Routine." (And you know it musta been a brother who sneaked that in.) For 50 years, Montague and his wife, Rose Thaddeus Casalan (known as Rose Catalon as a songwriter), acquired a collection of African American visual culture, historical artifacts, and documents, known as the Montague Collection. It's on display at the Meek-Eaton Black Archives Research Center and Museum of the Florida Agricultural and Mechanical University, in Tallahassee.

His autobiography, *Burn, Baby! Burn!* was published in October 2003 by the University of Illinois Press. Born in New Jersey, Montague rocked the mic in South LA and provided the most memorable phrase of the riot-filled 1960's and 1970's.

138

SOUTH LA'S LEADERS IN THE FIGHT FOR AFRICAN/BLACK PRIDE AND DIGNITY

CIVIL RIGHTS ACTIVISTS, COMMUNITY BUILDERS, FOUNDERS OF THE BLACK PANTHERS, BROTHERHOOD CRUSADE AND BLACK LIVES MATTER AND A REENTRY HERO

In Chapter Fourteen, we meet South LA's social justice warriors such as the founder of LA Black Panther Party, food and nutrition advocate, political strategist, and revolutionary leader, Alprentice "Bunchy" Carter; the first African American woman to run a major political campaign, and the main civil rights leader who pushed for the desegregation of LA City's swimming pools, Betty Hill; the first African American musician in a TV studio orchestra, and founder of an integrated musicians union, Buddy Collette; the fighter for equal access to public facilities, Dorothy Dandrige's body double, the you-know-she-must-have-been fine, Maggie Hathaway; the Afro-Mexicano founders of the pueblito now known as the City of Los Angeles, Los Pobladores; the co-founder of the Black Lives Matter movement, artist and social justice warrior, Patrice Cullors;the formerly incarcerated woman who has helped over 1,100 formerly incarcerated women find safety, hope and opportunity, the inspirational community re-integration leader, Susan Burton; and, the founder of LA's historic Black Congress and the nationally recognized Brotherhood Crusade of Los Angeles, Walter Bremond.

ALPRENTICE "BUNCHY" CARTER

FOUNDER OF THE SOUTHERN CALIFORNIA/LA CHAPTER OF THE BLACK PANTHER PARTY

(b. 1942 – d. 1969)

A civil rights-inspired social justice warrior, Alprentice "Bunchy" Carter had been exposed to crime early in life and served time in prison for armed robbery. During his incarceration, he joined the Nation of Islam. After returning home, Carter met Black Panther Party leaders and dedicated himself to the fight for black liberation, and joined the Black Panthers in 1967.

In 1968, after serving time, Carter became a founding member of the Southern California chapter of the Black Panther Party in LA. Under Carter's leadership, LA's Black Panthers studied politics, received training in firearms and first aid, and began the "Free Breakfast for Children" program. Later that year, the Panthers were admitting up to 100 new members a week, and a comprehensive and rigorous study of Black Panther literature, politics, firearms, and first-aid training was developed.

The presence of a skilled and disciplined black liberation movement in Los Angeles was unconscionable and intolerable to both the Los Angeles Police

Department and the Federal Bureau of Investigation. A campaign to under-
mine and ultimately destroy the panthers was launched. Beginning in 1969,
leaders of the Black Panther Party were targeted by the FBI COINTELPRO
program that assassinated, imprisoned, publicly humiliated, or falsely charged
Panthers and other activists with crimes. Born and raised in South LA, Carter
died, in the struggle, at a UCLA hospital.

BETTY HILL

THE WOMAN WHO DESEGREGATED LA CITY SWIMMING POOLS AND THE FIRST AFRICAN AMERICAN WOMAN TO RUN A MAJOR POLITICAL CAMPAIGN

(b. 1876 – d. 1960)

In the early 20th century, civil rights activist and top-notch political campaign manager Betty Hill was best known as "The Woman Who Desegregated LA's Public Pools," and respected in LA as a founding member of the Los Angeles NAACP. She was known as a leader in the fight for an end to all segregation in Los Angeles. Hill reached the pinnacle of her political career in 1932 when she ran the primary campaign for California Sen. Samuel M. Shortridge, becoming the first African American woman in the U.S. to run a major political campaign in the process.

Hill was a founding member of the LA chapter of the National Association for the Advancement of Colored People (NAACP), and the LA Urban League. She

was a Republican state central committeewoman for Southern California, a member of the National Council of Women; and a delegate to the 1940 Republican National Convention in Philadelphia (the first African American female west of the Rockies to serve as a delegate).

Hill's decades of activism and civic influence led the City of Los Angeles to honor her legacy by naming the Betty Hill Senior Citizen Center in her honor.

Founded in 2002, the Betty Hill Historical Foundation honors the legacy of a remarkable woman who believed that education is the key to achieving true equality and social justice. Hill's home, located in the West Jefferson neighborhood of South Los Angeles, was designated a Los Angeles Historic-Cultural Monument (#791) in 2005. Born in Nashville, Hill lived, fought segregationist laws, and died in South LA.

BUDDY COLLETTE

MASTER JAZZ MUSICIAN AND THE MAN WHO DESEGREGATED THE PROFESSIONAL MUSICIANS UNION

(b. 1921 – d. 2010)

When it comes to LA's unsung jazz heroes, Buddy Collette is as close to unmatched as it gets. A gifted composer and multi-instrumentalist, Collette continues to fly almost defiantly under the radar. An early pioneer at laying jazz on the flute and a leading figure in the 'bebop' and 'cool jazz' movements, Collette was also a civil rights activist and an important force in the LA jazz community. In 1933, at the age of 12, Collette formed his first jazz ensemble. The group contained a talented teenager named Charles Mingus, whom Collette convinced to switch from cello to bass. In 1949, Collette was the only African American member of the band for "You Bet Your Life," a TV and radio show hosted by Groucho Marx. In 1951, Collette became the first African American musician in a West Coast television studio band.

Discontented with being the only African American musician on TV, Collette became a leading activist against racism and discrimination in the music industry. In the early 1950s, he made concentrated efforts to form one, color-blind music union. In 1996, the United States Library of Congress honored

Collette by commissioning him to write and perform a special big-band concert highlighting his long career.

In June 2000, LA City councilmember Mark Ridley-Thomas called Collette "a living legend," and honored him with a "Living Museum" award. Collette was born in Watts, raised in Watts, and attended LA's Jordan High. He lived his entire life in South LA.

MAGGIE HATHAWAY

TALENTED ACTRESS, CIVIL RIGHTS LEADER AND FIGHTER FOR EQUAL ACCESS TO PUBLIC FACILITIES

(b. 1911 – d. 2001)

Best remembered as a civil rights activist, Maggie Hathaway had many talents, and left a memorable mark in radio, music, film, and civil rights. In Hollywood, Hathaway was a veteran of radio and film and contributed her talents and beauty, usually in small parts portraying sassy, sexy ladies, and helped open doors for other black actors and actresses. Disrespected and harassed by the male entertainment industry moguls, mass media, and police, she was described by them as militant and threatening.

Despite it all, Hathaway appeared in numerous movies and served as a body double for Dorothy Dandridge and Lena Horne—two of the most beautiful women to ever appear in film. During the civil rights movement, Hathaway began agitating against local golf courses which restricted African- American

patrons from usage. By 1958, she began writing a golf column in the California Eagle about black professional players.

In 1960, Hathaway organized the Minority Association for Golfers to support young African American golfers.

In 1963, Hathaway led a picket at the Long Beach municipal golf course to protest a lack of golf jobs for African American professional golfers.

In 1967, Hathaway co-founded the NAACP Image Awards. In 1994, Hathaway was inducted into the National Black Golf Hall of Fame. In 1997, the former Jack Thompson Golf Course located in Jesse Owens Park at 1921 West 98th Street, LA 90047 was rechristened the Maggie Hathaway Golf Course in her honor. Born in Louisiana, Hathaway lived, served, and died in South LA.

LOS POBLADORES

AFRICAN, INDIGENOUS AND LATINO FOUNDERS OF LOS ANGELES

(Founded 1781)

On Sept. 4, 1781, after an over 1,100 mile-long trek north, Los Pobladores, 44 original settlers and 4 soldiers, founded the city of LA officially named "El Pueblo de Nuestra Señora la Reina de los Ángeles de Porciúncula,"—"The Town of Our Lady the Queen of the Angels of Porciúncula."

According to early stories, only two of the 44 were white, 26 were African and 16 were indigenous. Later, the multiracial ethnicity of Los Pobladores which had been rejected as rumors by the scholarly establishment, was never accepted until explicit census information was found in an archive in Seville, Spain. Spanish colonial census documents confirmed the race/ethnicity of the 11 families recruited by Felipe de Neve, the first Spanish governor of California, and that they arrived from the Mexican provinces of Sinaloa and Sonora.

In the 1950's, a plaque was installed in El Pueblo de Los Angeles State Historic Park paying tribute; but there are no grandiose monuments, no streets or landmarks named for the 44 African, Afro-Latino and indigenous founders of LA.

PATRISSE CULLORS

#BLACKLIVESMATTER CREATOR & CO-FOUNDER OF THE BLACK LIVES MATTER MOVEMENT

(b. 1983)

Artist and social justice warrior, Patrisse Cullors—along with community organizers and friends Alicia Garza and Opal Tometi—founded Black Lives Matter. The three started the movement out of frustration over George Zimmerman's acquittal in the shooting of Trayvon Martin. In 2013, Cullors created the hashtag #BlackLivesMatter to corroborate Garza's use of the phrase in making a Facebook post about Trayvon Martin after his murder by George Zimmerman. The movement has since expanded into an international organization with dozens of chapters around the world campaigning against anti-black racism.

Cullors' work for Black Lives Matter recently received recognition in Time magazine's 100 Most Influential People of 2020 list and Time magazine's 2020 "100 Women of the Year." In January 2016, Patrisse Cullors published her memoir, When They Call You a Terrorist: A Black Lives Matter Memoir, which became a New York Times bestseller. From 2016 to 2018 Patrisse

worked as a senior fellow at MomsRising, where she worked on ground-breaking federal legislation that will change the outcomes of maternal mortality for women, especially black women. Cullors credits social media as being instrumental in revealing violence against African Americans, saying: "On a daily basis, every moment, black folks are being bombarded with images of our death." In 2020, Cullors received a Durfee Stanton Fellowship to further her efforts. Cullors was born, raised, and resides in South LA.

SUSAN BURTON

REENTRY HERO AND FIGHTER FOR FORMERLY INCARCERATED WOMEN

(b. Unknown)

In 1998, Susan Burton founded A New Way of Life Reentry Project in Watts, a Los Angeles-based non-profit that provides formerly incarcerated women with housing and supportive services. Burton had been cycling in and out of prison for nearly two decades on drug-related convictions after suffering memories of sexual abuse as a child, and the death of her five-year-old son led to addiction and despair.

Following her last term in prison, Burton gained her sobriety at the CLARE Foundation in Santa Monica in October 1997. Wondering why South Los Angeles didn't offer similar services, Burton opened up her own home to women who had just left prison and needed a place to live. Today, A New Way of Life has eight safe homes in Los Angeles and Long Beach, where more than 1,100 formerly incarcerated women have found safety, hope, and opportunity.

On August 29, 2019, Susan Burton, was issued a full pardon by Governor Gavin Newsom. According to a statement from Newsom's office, the pardon "does not minimize past conduct, it recognizes a person's subsequent progress and accomplishments. A pardon does not expunge or erase the conviction." Burton was originally granted a certificate of rehabilitation by the Superior Court of California in 2004.

Burton was named a CNN Hero in 2010, a Purpose Prize winner in 2012, Leadership Award in 2014, and 2015 and an honorary Doctor of Humane Letters degree from CSU Northridge in 2019. Burton's autobiography, *Becoming Ms. Burton: From Prison to Recovery to Leading the Fight for Incarcerated Women* was published in 2017. Born and raised in the city, Burton continues to serve South LA.

WALTER BREMOND

FOUNDED LA BLACK CONGRESS AND THE BROTHERHOOD CRUSADE OF LOS ANGELES

(b. 1934 — d. 1982)

Mr. Bremond, a native of Austin, Tex., earned a Bachelor of Arts degree and a Master of Science degree from San Francisco State College, and became active in the black community of South LA. In 1962 organized the LA Black Congress. In 1968, in the aftermath of the Watts riots, Bremond founded the Brotherhood Crusade of Los Angeles, which has grown into an over 50-year-old grassroots organization with a vision of improving quality of life and meeting the unmet needs of low-income, underserved, under-represented and disenfranchised individuals.

In 1974, Mr. Bremond moved to New York and founded the National Black United Fund (NBUF) in Manhattan.

In 1976 NBUF scored a major victory when a federal court ruled that it, and other minority charities, could raise funds through payroll deductions from federal employees. Bremond's belief was that African Americans  "had a responsibility to assist in our own growth and development, that we could not forever go to the larger white community and ask for support of programs we believe are important for our survival without doing something ourselves." Born in Texas, Bremond raised his family in South LA and died in New York City at the age of 48.

SOUTH LA'S ALTERNATIVE SPIRITUALISTS

A PAN AFRICAN ORCHESTRA FOUNDER, AN ARCHBISHOP AND AN EVANGELIST

In Chapter Fifteen, we learn a little about South LA's significant impacts on religion and spirituality, and we meet three of the remarkable spiritual forces who made them such as the former Motown records singer turned religious leader, Archbishop Carl Bean, the founder of America's first LGBTQ affirming and welcoming African American church; the Founder Pan Afrikan Peoples Arkestra and The Union of God's Musicians and Artists Ascension, a group composed of South LA musicians focused on the explicit goal of expanding Pan-African spiritual consciousness through music, Horace Elva Tapscott; and, the man who inspired over 10,000 people to speak in tongues, evangelist, and leader of the "Azusa Street Revival," and founder of what became the world-wide Pentecostalist movement, William Seymour.

ARCHBISHOP CARL BEAN

RELIGIOUS FREEDOM FOR LGBTQ COMMUNITY AND ACCESS TO AIDS SERVICES

(b. 1944 — d. 2021)

In 1982, Carl Bean, a former Motown musician, founded America's first affirming and welcoming African American church—the Unity Fellowship Church Movement—for the LGBTQ community. The South Los Angeles-based church grew into a movement that eventually went national and is heralded as the first black church for LGBT persons.

In 1985, Bean founded the Minority AIDS Project (MAP) in South LA to address the needs of individuals within the African American and Latino communities who were living with HIV/AIDS. Since then, MAP has provided a wide range of services involving prevention, and care, and treatment services for low-income people of color at high risk of HIV infection or transmission within the South LA community.

On May 26, 2019, then LA City Council President Herb Wesson designated the intersection of Jefferson Blvd. and Sycamore Ave. as "Archbishop Carl Bean Square" for the founder of Minority AIDS Project and the Unity Fellowship Church Movement, America's first affirming and welcoming African American church for lesbian, gay, bisexual and transgender persons. Born in Baltimore, Bean lived, created a church, provided spiritual leadership, and helped the poor, sick, and needy in South LA.

HORACE ELVA TAPSCOTT

FOUNDER OF THE PAN AFRIKAN PEOPLES ARKESTRA AND THE UNION OF GOD'S MUSICIANS

(b. 1934 – d. 1999)

In 1961, Horace Tapscott founded the Pan Afrikan Peoples Arkestra in Watts. Tapscott's goal was to depict "The lives of black people in their communities all over the country, where it had been turned around and been just made to fit the mode of being black and unworthy. We were trying to kill that kind of attitude about black folks through art."

In 1963, Tapscott formed the Underground Musicians Association/Union of God's Musicians and Artists Ascension with the goal of making music that brought folks together and eased tensions between groups, creating spaces so that the people had a place to turn to when they needed help, heightening social awareness.

Tapscott wrote that African Americans have "a rich history to be proud of and that re-education was needed to make that apparent." Tapscott's musical mission was to preserve, develop and perform black music and create an understanding of togetherness and harmony that would produce empowerment through music. This empowerment could then be harnessed in the fight for freedom.

Tapscott's music reflects everyday life and the experience of the musician. Tapscott's work is the subject of the UCLA Horace Tapscott Jazz Collection. Born in Houston, Texas, Tapscott was raised and lived in the Watts community of South LA.

WILLIAM SEYMOUR

EVANGELIST, FOUNDER OF PENTECOSTALISM

(b. 1870 – d. 1922)

In 1906, Evangelist William Seymour moved to Los Angeles, California, where he preached the Pentecostal message and sparked the Azusa Street Revival in downtown LA—an influential event in the rise of the Pentecostal and other charismatic movements. The LA-based revival, recognized by Pentacostals as the first incident of speaking-in-tongues, drew large crowds of believers as well as media coverage that focused on the controversial religious practices and the racially integrated worship services, which violated the racial norms of the time and upset racists. Seymour's leadership of the revival and publication of *The Apostolic Faith* newspaper launched him into prominence within the young Pentecostal movement.

Under his leadership, the Azusa Street Mission sent evangelists throughout the United States, spreading the Pentecostal message from Los Angeles

all over the United States and resulting in many missions that modeled themselves after Azusa. By 1907, missionaries from Azusa Street had reached Mexico, Canada, Western Europe, the Middle East, West Africa, and parts of Asia.

By 1914, Pentecostalism had spread to almost every major U.S. city. All major American Pentecostal denominations can trace their origins to Azusa Street, including the Assemblies of God, the Church of God in Christ, the Church of God (Cleveland, Tennessee), the Pentecostal Assemblies of the World, the United Pentecostal Church, and the Pentecostal Holiness Church. Born in Louisiana, Seymour inspired, lived, and died in South LA.

SOUTH LA'S AFRICAN AMERICAN SPORT STARS

FOOTBALL STARS, OLYMPIANS, A PIONEERING GOLFER AND A HALL OF FAME HOOPSTER

In Chapter Sixteen, we meet seven African American sports stars from South LA including the man who fought segregation in the sport of golf—paving the way for Charlie Sifford, Lee Elder and Tiger Woods, Bill Spiller; the woman who—by winning NCAA, WNBA AND Olympic championships—established herself as one of the best basketball players on the planet, Cynthia Cooper; the Fastest Woman of All Time—talented, beautiful and unique—Florence Griffith Joyner; the 1932 Berlin Olympics bronze medalist, scientist and scholar, James LuValle; the first African American in the National Football League (NFL) in the modern era, Kenny Washington; sprinter, triple gold medalist and home-grown star of the 1984 Los Angeles Olympics, Valerie Brisco Hooks; the second African American in the NFL and star of Hollywood western movies, Woodrow Strode.

BILL SPILLER

FIRST SUCCESSFUL AFRICAN AMERICAN GOLFER, FOUGHT RACISM AND SEGREGATION IN GOLF

(b. 1913 – d. 1988)

A professional golfer who helped successfully advocate for the inclusion of African Americans in Professional Golfing Association (PGA) Tour events, Spiller did not learn to golf until the age of thirty in December of 1942. However, he quickly learned the game, and turned pro in 1947 by joining the African American United Golfers Association tour. At the 1948 LA Open, Spiller was tied with the accomplished golfer Ben Hogan but faltered in later rounds. As a late-bloomer, Spiller spent many years challenging the segregation policy of the Professional Golfers Association of America.

Angered by the racism that had limited his life since childhood—and discouraged by his inability to overcome that racism to achieve the success that he believed he had earned—Spiller remained bitter toward the white golfing

establishment until his death. However, enormous societal changes had begun with these small acts of resistance, and the difficult work done by Spiller and other black golfers to challenge the "Caucasian-only" Professional Golfers' Association broke the race barrier in golf and helped also show that a segregated elitist sport could also be desegregated. laid the groundwork for athletes of color in all sports for decades to come.

In the end, Spiller was successful in advocating for the inclusion of African Americans in public golfing events and is widely recognized as the most responsible for Africans Americans being admitted to join the PGA. Born in Tishomingo, Oklahoma, Spiller lived and died in South LA.

CYNTHIA COOPER-DYKE

HIGH SCHOOL, NCAA, WNBA, AND OLYMPIC BASKETBALL CHAMPION

(b. 1963)

In basketball, Hall of Famer Cynthia Cooper-Dyke has accomplished just about everything. In 1981, she helped the Locke High Saints (Watts, CA) win the California state basketball championship and was named Los Angeles player of the year; in 1983, she led the USC Trojans to a National Collegiate Basketball Association (NCAA) championship; in 1984, she won another NCAA championship and led the United States in winning the Olympic gold medal; and, in 1986 and 1990, she led the United States to consecutive world basketball championships.

As a Women's National Basketball Association (WNBA) professional, Cooper-Dyke led the Houston Comets to four WNBA championships (i.e.,1997, 1998, 1999, 2000) and was named Most Valuable Player (MVP) in each series. In 1997 she was recognized as the WNBA MVP. In 1998, in addition to repeating as WNBA MVP, the Women's Sports Foundation selected Cooper-Dyke, Sportswoman of the Year.

In 2004, when Cooper-Dyke retired she led the WNBA in all career scoring categories. In 2009, she was inducted into the Women's Basketball Hall of Fame and, in 2010, the Naismith Hall of Fame. Cooper-Dyke's biography She Got Game: My Personal Odyssey covers her childhood, her basketball career and her mother's breast cancer battle. Cooper-Dyke was born in Chicago and raised in Watts.

FLORENCE GRIFFITH-JOYNER

FASTEST WOMAN OF ALL-TIME

(b. 1959 – d. 1998)

Upon Florence Griffith-Joyner's unexpected death in 1988, then-President Bill Clinton said, "We were dazzled by her speed, humbled by her talent and captivated by her style." Young Florence Griffith began racing when she was seven years old, joined the Sugar Ray Robinson Organization when she was in elementary school, won the Jesse Owens National Youth Games two years in a row at the ages of 14 and 15, and ran track at Jordan High School in Watts.

However, she was forced to give up sport at nineteen to help support her family. Sprint coach Bob Kersee found her working as a bank teller and helped her enroll at UCLA. In 1983, Griffith graduated from UCLA with her bachelor's degree in psychology. On July 6, 1988, in the U.S. Olympic Trials, Griffith Joyner achieved a stunning breakthrough when she ran the 100m in 10.49 seconds, obliterating Evelyn Ashford's record of 10.79. Her time was faster than the men's records in a wide range of countries, including Ireland, New Zealand, Norway and Turkey.

Known as Flo-Jo the world over, Joyner won three gold medals at the 1988 Olympics and her 1988 World Record in the 100-and-200-meter competitions

still stands and she remains the Fastest Woman of All Time. Flo-Jo received a slew of awards for her transcendent performances. In 1988, Flo-Jo was named the Associated Press Female Athlete of the Year.

In 1989, Flo-Jo won Germany's Golden Camera award for her performance in the 1988 Seoul Olympics and a USA Kids' Choice Award for "Favorite Female Athlete." Born in LA and raised in the Jordan Downs Housing Project in Watts, Flo-Jo electrified South LA.

JAMES LUVALLE

OLYMPIC ATHLETE, SCIENTIST, AND FIRST AFRICAN AMERICAN TO EARN A PHD. FROM CALTECH

(b. 1912 — d. 1993)

In the summer of 1936, James LuValle earned a B.A. in chemistry from the University of California Los Angeles (UCLA), won the 400 meter Olympic bronze medal in the historic Berlin games and gained the nickname 'the Olympic Chemist.' In 1937, LuValle returned to UCLA, earned a M.A. in chemistry and physics, and founded the UCLA Graduate Students Association.

In 1940, LuValle became the first African American to earn a Ph.D. (chemistry and mathematics) from the California Institute of Technology (CalTech) and accepted a position at historically-black, Fisk University. Later, he worked for Kodak's research labs, as a senior scientist and head of photographic chemistry for Fairfield Space Defense Systems and as scientific coordinator for Palo Alto Research and Engineering.

During his career, LuValle published over 30 peer-reviewed scientific articles and held eight U.S. patents. In 1985, UCLA named the new student center, LuValle Commons, in his honor. In 1987 he was honored by CalTech with the Alumni Distinguished Service Award and by UCLA's Professional Achievement Award. Born in San Antonio, Texas, LuValle moved to South LA as a child. excelled academically and athletically, and died in New Zealand while on vacation.

In 1985, the Associated Students of UCLA named its new student center LuValle Commons in his honor. In 1987, LuValle received the Alumni Distinguished Service Award from California Institute of Technology and the Professional Achievement Award from UCLA. Born in San Antonio, LuValle moved to South LA while in elementary school, was raised in South LA, excelled academically and athletically, and died on vacation in New Zealand.

KENNY WASHINGTON

FIRST AFRICAN AMERICAN IN THE NATIONAL FOOTBALL LEAGUE IN THE MODERN ERA

(b. 1918 – d. 1971)

In 1946, UCLA's Kenny Washington became the first African American in the National Football League (NFL) in the modern era.

From its inception in 1899 all the way through 1932, the NFL was an integrated operation and many teams were multi-ethnic with African American, Asian-American, Latin-American and Native-American players on their rosters. However, in 1933, George Marshall, the openly racist owner of the Boston Braves baseball club and the Washington Redskins football club, pressured the other NFL owners to ban African American athletes and institute a strict segregation policy.

With the NFL's Los Angeles (LA) Rams were facing eviction from the LA Coliseum unless they ceased segregationist practices and signed an African American player, the Rams, and the NFL, responded by lifting the discriminatory ban.

On March 21, 1946, the Rams signed Kenny Washington making him the first African American in the National Football League (NFL) in the modern era.

 Shortly afterwards, the Rams signed Washington's former UCLA teammate, Woodrow Strode making him the second African American in the NFL. Later, in 1956, Washington was inducted into the College Football Hall of Fame and honored by the LA Memorial Coliseum Commission for his role in dismantling segregation.

Born and raised in South LA, Washington attended Lincoln High and UCLA. Washington suffered from heart and lung problems and died in South LA at the age of 52.

VALERIE BRISCO HOOKS

FIRST OLYMPIAN TO WIN THE 200 METER AND 400 METER RACE IN THE SAME OLYMPICS

(b. 1960)

In the 1984 Los Angeles Olympics, South LA's Valerie Brisco-Hooks electrified the sports world when she won gold medals in the 200 meter and 400 meter Olympic final - accomplishing a feat that no athlete, male or female, had ever achieved. Her 400 meter time broke the Olympic record and still ranks as the tenth fastest performance of all-time. Brisco-Hooks capped her Olympic performance by winning a third gold medal with the U.S. women's 4x400 meter relay team. In the 1988 Seoul Olympics, she won a silver medal with the U.S. women's 4x400 meter relay team. In 1995, Brisco-Hooks was inducted into the U.S. Track and Field Hall of Fame. Currently, Brisco-Hooks coaches with Bob Kersee and works with athletes at West LA College.

Brisco-Hooks was born in Greenwood, Mississippi, raised in Watts, attended West Athens Elementary, Locke High and Cal State Northridge and continues to reside in south LA.

WOODY STRODE

OLYMPIAN, FOOTBALL STAR AND MOVIE STAR

(b. 1914 – d. 1994)

In 1946, after playing football alongside Kenny Washington, running track with future LA Mayor Tom Bradley at UCLA, and appearing in the 1936 Berlin Olympics Games, Woodrow Wilson Strode - better known as Woody - followed Kenny Washington, his former UCLA football teammate, in signing with the LA Rams. In the process, Strode became the second African American in the National Football League in the postwar era. While Stode and Washington were breaking barriers in football, Jackie Robinson, their former teammate at UCLA and in the semi-professional Pacific Coast Professional Football League, would go on to break the so-called color barrier in professional baseball.

Strode, a Black Indian (his grandmother was Black Cherokee and his grandfather was Black Muscogee), was born and raised in South LA, attended Jefferson High, starred in football, track and Hollywood films. Strode died in Glendora, CA.

ACKNOWLEDGMENTS

I would like to acknowledge my amazing wife, Manal. Your love, support and input—from the early conceptual conversations on content and organization to reading transcripts to profile editing—and your encouragement throughout, were essential. You were there for me at every stage of the book. Thank you. You are there for me for everything and still make the best soup that I ever tasted. I love you.

I would like to acknowledge my sons, Taj and Sadiq. I love you. Being your father is my greatest achievement because, I believe, the greatness inside of you will be expressed through you or through your progeny. I'm so proud of who you guys are. Just like the remarkable people profiled in this book, you had the good luck of being born and raised in South LA. The rest of it is up to you. Go forth, be fair, be frugal, be honest, be steadfast, be trustworthy, do your best, and stay physically fit.

I would like to acknowledge Marina Scott. Thank you for helping me through the entire process of conceptualizing my research in book format, designing the book cover/jacket design and interior layout, preparing the book for publication, setting up distribution vehicles and website design. Your help has been invaluable. You are very smart, your work is high quality, and I give you the highest of recommendations. It has been great working with you.

Last, I would like to acknowledge my mother, Lillian, for giving birth to me and raising me in South LA.

PHOTO CREDITS

APPENDIX

Born in South LA documented the stories, struggles, accomplishments and events of significance of over 100 remarkable African Americans who were born, raised, lived or died in South LA, California. Read this appendix to find examples of their work (i.e., anthologies, biographies, books, discographies, documentaries, filmographies, interviews, plays, soundtracks and TV appearances) and learn more about their unique contributions to Black History and the South LA community.

A.C. Bilbrew

Albums: *An Evening With AC Bilbrew* (Unknown).

Poetry: *The Creation* (1960), *Amen Chorus* (1960).

Films: *Hearts in Dixie* (1929).

Alprentice "Bunchy" Carter

Documentaries: *The Black Panthers:Vanguard of the Revolution* (2015), *Black History at UCLA: Bunchy Carter and the Black Panthers* (2017).

Arnaud "Arna" Bontemps

Books: *God Sends Sunday* (1931), *Black Thunder* (1936).

Plays: *St. Louis Woman* (1946), *Free and Easy* (1949).

Augustus Freeman Hawkins

Interviews: *Interview with Augustus Hawkins,* conducted by Blackside, Inc. (1992).

Documents: *Augustus F. Hawkins Papers* (1935-1990).

Beulah Woodard

Sculptures: *Maudelle* (ca. 1937–38), *Bad Boy* (1937), *Biddy Mason* (ca. 1949).

Paintings: *African Woman* (ca. 1935).

Bill Spiller

Biographies: *Forbidden Fairways* (1998), *A Course of Their Own* (2000), *Game of Privilege: An African American History of Golf* (2017).

'Black Belt Jones' (Fictional Character)

Film: *Black Belt Jones directed by Robert Clouse* (1974).

Soundtrack: *Theme from Black Belt Jones by Dennis Coffey and Luchi De Jesus* (1974).

Brenda Sykes

TV Appearances: *Black Gunn* (1972), *Ozzie's Girls* (1973), *Cleopatra Jones* (1973), *Mandingo* (1975).

Bridget 'Biddy' Mason

Biographical Articles: *Biddy Mason and the Founding of Los Angeles: From Slavery to Entrepreneurship* by KCET (2020), *Bridget "Biddy" Mason* by National Park Services (2021).

Documentaries: *One Of The First African American Millionaires and Her Impact On Los Angeles* by University of California Television (2019).

Buddy Collette

Albums: *Man of Many Parts* (1956), *Jazz Loves Paris* (1958), *Tasty Dish* (2004).

Calafia (Fictional Character)

Books: *The Adventures of Esplandián* (ca. 1510).

Carl Bean (Archbishop)

Autobiography: *I Was Born This Way* (2010).

Songs: *I Was Born This Way* (1975).

Charles Mingus

Autobiography: *Beneath the Underdog* (1971).

Biography: *Tonight at Noon* (2002).

Charles Wright

Songs: Do *Your Thing* (1968), *Till You Get Enough* (1969), *Express Yourself* (1970).

174

Charlotta Bass

Documents: *Charlotta A. Bass Papers* (1924-1983).

Chester Himes

Books: *If He Hollers Let Him Go* (1945), *Harlem Detective Series* (1957-1969).

Autobiographies: *The Quality of Hurt: The Autobiography of Chester Himes* (1971), *My Life of Absurdity: The Autobiography of Chester Himes* (1972).

Chester Washington

Editorials: *Chester Washington commentary re Wendell poll* (1939).

Namesakes: *Chester Washington Golf Course* (1928-)

Cynthia Cooper

Autobiography: *She Got Game: My Personal Odyssey* (1999).

Filmography: *She Ball* (2020).

Dexter Gordon

Albums: *Go* (1962), *More Than You Know* (1975), *The Other Side of Round Midnight* (1986).

Biography: *Sophisticated Giant: The Life and Legacy of Dexter Gordon* (2018).

Documentary: *Dexter Gordon: More Than You Know* (1996).

Diane Watson

Documents: *Diane E. Watson Papers* (1978-2011).

Dorothy Dandridge

Filmography: *Carmen Jones* (1954), *Porgy and Bess* (1959).

Biographical Films: *Introducing Dorothy Dandridge* (1999).

Eddie 'Rochester' Anderson

Filmography: *Cabin in the Sky* (1943), *The Jack Benny Program* (1950-1965).

Elvira 'Vi' Redd

Albums: *Bird Call* (1962), *Lady Soul* (1963).

Biographical Articles: *Invisible Woman: Vi Redd's Contributions as a Jazz Saxophonist* (2013).

Documentaries: *Styles of Jazz Featuring Vi Redd* (1981).

Etta James

Songs: *At Last* (1961), *Something's Got a Hold on Me* (1962), *Tell Mama* (1967).

Autobiography: *A Rage to Survive* (1995).

Ezekiel "Easy" Porterhouse Rawlins (Fictional Character)

Book: *Devil in A Blue Dress by Walter Mosley* (1990).

Film: *Devil in a Blue Dress* written and directed by Carl Franklin (1995).

Ferdinand Jelly Roll Morton

Songs: *Jelly Roll Blues* (2015), *King Porter Stomp* (1923), *Black Bottom Stomp* (1925).

Biography: *Mister Jelly Roll* (1950).

Florence Cole Talbert

Recordings: *Bell Song* (1923), *The Last Rose of Summer* (1923).

Famous Roles: *Aida* (ca. 1927-1930).

Florence Griffith-Joyner

Footage: *Florence Griffith-Joyner- The Fastest Woman of All-Time by Olympics* (2020).

Frederick Madison Roberts

Documents: *Roberts Family Papers* (1853-1994).

Gerald Wilson

Albums: *California Soul* (1968), *State Street Sweet* (1994), *New York, New Sound* (2003).

Biography: *The Jazz Pilgrimage of Gerald Wilson* (2018)

Hadda Brooks

Albums: *Queen of the Boogie* (1984), *Anytime, Anyplace, Anywhere* (1994).

Interviews: *Hadda Brooks TV Interview with Host Skip E Lowe* (1994).

Hampton Hawes

Albums: *Here and Now* (1965), Playin' in the Yard (1973).

Autobiography: *Raise Up Off Me* (1974).

Horace Elva Tapscott

Albums: *The Giant is Awakened* (1969), *Flight 17* (1978), *The Dark Tree* (1991).

Composer Credits in Films: *Leimert Park: The Story of a Village in South Central Los Angeles* (2006), *As Above, So Below* (1973).

Issa Rae

Filmography: *The Misadventures of Awkward Black Girl* (2011-2013), *Little* (2019), *Insecure* (2016-).

Memoir: *The Misadventures of Awkward Black Girl* (2015).

Ivie Anderson

Recordings: *It Don't Mean a Thing (If It Ain't Got That Swing)* (1932), *Stormy Weather* (1940).

Filmography: *A Day at the Races* (1937), *The Hit Parade* (1937).

James LuValle

Transcribed Interview: *An Olympian's Oral History: Dr. James E. LuValle, 1936 Olympic Track & Field* (1988).

Biography: *Olympic Pride, American Prejudice: The Untold Story of 17 African Americans Who Defied Jim Crow and Adolf Hitler to Compete in the 1936 Berlin Olympics* (2020).

Janet Collins

Biography: *Night's Dancer: The Life of Janet Collins* (2011).

Filmography: *Flamingo* (1942), *Carmen* (1952), *The Admiral Broadway Revue* (1949).

Jody Watley

Songs: *Looking for a New Love* (1987), *Don't You Want Me* (1987), *Real Love* (1989).

Soundtrack Credits: *Die Hard* (1990), *Pose* (2018-).

John Neimore

Archived Newspaper Content: *California Eagle Photograph Collection* (Late 1800s -Late 1950s).

John Outterbridge

Artworks: *The Containment Series* (1968), *Dreads* (2011).

Interviews: *Beyond Vernacular: An Interview with John Outterbridge* (2013).

John Singleton

Filmography: *Boyz n the Hood* (1991), *Rosewood* (1997), *Shaft* (2000), *2 Fast 2 Furious* (2003).

Johnnie Cochran

Autobiography: *A Lawyer's Life* (2001).

Documentary: *Johnnie Cochran's Journey* (2002).

Filmography: *Arli$$* (1998), *JAG* (2000), *Showtime* (2002).

Kenny Washington

Documentary: *Forgotten Four: The Integration of Pro Football* (2014).

Filmography: *Rope of Sand* (1949), *Pinky* (1949), *The Jackie Robinson Story* (1950).

Leon H. Washington

Archived Newspapers: *Los Angeles Sentinel Newspaper Collection* (1934-2005).

Leonard Stovall

Legacy: Stovall Foundation (est. 1957).

Lester Young

Albums: *Pres and Sweets* (1956), *The Jazz Giants '56* (1956), *Laughin' to Keep from Cryin'* (1959).

Biography: Being Prez: *The Life and Music of Lester Young* (2007).

Louise Beavers

Filmography: *Imitation of Life* (1934), *Holiday Inn* (1942), *Beulah* (1952).

Madame Sul-Te-Wan

Filmography: *Maid of Salem* (1937), I*n Old Chicago* (1938), *Safari* (1940).

Magnificent Montague

Autobiography: *Burn, Baby! Burn!* (2003).

Interviews: *The Magnificent Montague: 'Burn Baby Burn'* NPR (2003).

Songs: *The Montague Theme* (Unknown).

Maggie Hathaway

Biography: *A Tearful Journey For Freedom: The Life and Times of Maggie Hathaway* (2003).

Marla Gibbs

Filmography: *The Jeffersons* (1975–1985), 227 (1985–1990), *Martin* (1995).

Marvin Gaye

Albums: *How Sweet It Is to Be Loved by You* (1965), *I Heard It Through the Grapevine* (1968), *What's Going On* (1971).

Biography: *Divided Soul: The Life of Marvin Gaye* (1985).

Documentary: *What's Going On: The Marvin Gaye Story* (2006).

Maxine Waters

Documents: *Maxine Waters papers* (1976-1990).

Melba Liston

Albums: *Melba Liston and Her 'Bones* (1959), *Volcano Blues* (1993).

Composer Credits: *Smile Orange* (1976).

Minnie Riperton

Songs: *Lovin' You* (1974), *Inside My Love* (1975), *Memory Lane* (1979).

Documentary: *Unsung* (2008).

Miriam Matthews

Collections: *Miriam Matthews Photograph Collection* (1781-1989).

Interviews: *Black Women Oral History Project Interviews with Miriam Matthews* (1977).

Natalie Cole

Albums: *Natalie* (1976), *Unpredictable* (1977), *Unforgettable... with Love* (1991).

Autobiography: *Angel on My Shoulder* (2000).

Films: *Livin' for Love: The Natalie Cole Story* (2000).

Nipsey Hussle

Album: *Victory Lap* (2018).

Mixtapes: *The Marathon* (2010), *The Marathon Continues* (2011), *Crenshaw* (2013).

Biography: *The Marathon Don't Stop: The Life and Times of Nipsey Hussle* (2021).

Patrice Rushen

Songs: *Haven't You Heard* (1980), *Forget Me Nots* (1982)

Soundtrack Credits: *Hollywood Shuffle* (1987), *Men in Black* (1997).

Patrisse Cullors

Books: *When They Call You a Terrorist: A Black Lives Matter Memoir* (2018).

Documentary: *Stay Woke: The Black Lives Matter Movement* (2016).

Paul Beatty

Novels: *The White Boy Shuffle* (1996), *The Sellout* (2015).

Poetry Books: *Big Bank Take Little Bank* (1991), *Joker, Joker, Deuce* (1994).

Paul R. Williams

Books: *The Small Home of Tomorrow* (1945), *New Homes for Today* (1946).

Documentary: *Paul Williams - A Legend in Architecture* (2007).

Ralph Bunche

Books: *World View of Race* (1936), *The Political Status of the Negro in the Age of FDR* (1973).

Documents: *Ralph J. Bunche Papers* (1927-1971).

Richard Wyatt

Artwork: *Hollywood Jazz: 1945-1972* (1991), *City of Dreams/River of History Mural* (1996).

Rita Walters:

Interviews: *UCLA Libraries Center for Oral Research, Interview with Rita Walters* (2008).

Robert Owens:

Articles: *Pioneering Black Urbanites in San Francisco and Los Angeles, California Historical Society* (2019).

Roy Ayers

Albums: *Everybody Loves the Sunshine* (1976), *Vibrations* (1976).

Performance Videos: *Roy Ayers: NPR Music Tiny Desk Concert* (2018).

Susan Burton

Autobiography: *Becoming Ms. Burton: From Prison to Recovery to leading the Fight for Incarcerated Women* (2017).

TedxTalk: *Providing Formerly Incarcerated Women with a New Way of Life* (2018).

Teresa Graves

Filmography: *Our Place* (1967), *Rowan & Martin's Laugh-In* (1969–1970), *Get Christie Love!* (1974–1975).

Tom Bradley

Biographies: *The Black Bruins: The Remarkable Lives of UCLA's Jackie Robinson, Woody Strode, Tom Bradley, Kenny Washington, and Ray Bartlett* (2018).

Documents: *Mayor Tom Bradley Administration Papers* (1920-1993).

Valerie Brisco Hooks

Footage: *200 Meter US Olympic Trials* (1984), *Valerie Brisco Hooks Olympic 400 Meter Final* (1984).

Walter Mosley

Books: *Devil in a Blue Dress* (1990), *The Long Fall* (2009), *Charcoal Joe* (2016).

Plays: *The Fall of Heaven* (2011), *Lift* (2014)

Filmography: *Fallen Angels: Fearless* (1995), *Snowfall* (2018-2020).

Wanda Coleman

Books: *Wicked Enchantment: Selected Poems* (2020).

Interviews: *Wanda Coleman Poetry. LA Interview* (2013).

Wendy Raquel Robinson

FIlmography: *The Steve Harvey Show* (1996–2002), *The Game* (2006–2015), *Grand Hotel* (2019).

William Seymour

Biographies: *William J Seymour-Pioneer of the Azusa Street Revival* (2012).

Dcumentary: *The Azusa Street Project* (2006).

William Grant Still

Articles: *Get to Know: William Grant Still, Jr.,* by LA Phil (Unknown).

Compositions: *Afro-American Symphony* (1930), *Troubled Island* (1949), *A Bayou Legend* (1974).

Interview: *An Interview with the Afro-American Composer William Grant Still,* by Voice of America (Unknown).

Woody Strode

Autobiography: *Goal Dust* (1990).

Filmography: *Sergeant Rutledge* (1960), S*partacus* (1960), *The Man Who Shot Liberty Valance* (1962).

Yvonne Brathwaite Burke (YBB)

Documents: *Yvonne Brathwaite Burke Papers* (1968-2008).

REFERENCES

AC Bilbrew:

https://www.nps.gov/nr/feature/afam/2010/Cover-AfricanAmericansinLA.pdf;

https://en.wikipedia.org/wiki/A._C._Bilbrew;

Alprentice 'Bunchy' Carter:

https://en.wikipedia.org/wiki/Bunchy_Carter;

https://en.wikipedia.org/wiki/COINTELPRO;

Arnaud 'Arna' Bontemps:

https://www.nps.gov/nr/feature/afam/2010/Cover-AfricanAmericansinLA.pdf;

https://en.wikipedia.org/wiki/Arna_Bontemps;

Aquanetta Warren:

https://achieve.lausd.net/cms/lib/CA01000043/Centricity/Domain/599/LAUSD%20Alumni%20History%20and%20Hall%20of%20Fame.pdf; page 208;

Augustus Hawkins:

https://history.house.gov/People/Detail/14733;

https://www.nps.gov/nr/feature/afam/2010/Cover-AfricanAmericansinLA.pdf; Appendix II;

https://en.wikipedia.org/wiki/Augustus_Hawkins;

Barbara Boudreaux:

https://www.latimes.com/archives/la-xpm-1997-01-08-me-16443-story.html;

L.A. School Board Member Finalizes Plan for Ebonics;

https://www.latimes.com/archives/la-xpm-1997-01-08-me-16443-story.html;

https://www.latimes.com/archives/la-xpm-1995-02-17-me-33064-story.html;

http://www.lausd.k12.ca.us/lausd/board/boudreaux.html;

Beulah Woodard:

https://www.nps.gov/nr/feature/afam/2010/Cover-AfricanAmericansinLA.pdf

https://en.wikipedia.org/wiki/Beulah_Woodard;

https://www.askart.com/artist/Beulah_Ecton_Woodard/10059527/Beulah_Ecton_Woodard.aspx;

Bessie Burke:

https://www.nps.gov/people/bessieburke.htm;

https://www.nps.gov/nr/feature/afam/2010/Cover-AfricanAmericansinLA.pdf

Betty Hill:

https://lacontroller.org/data-stories-and-maps/African American-heritage-map/;

https://la.curbed.com/2019/8/19/20757888/betty-hill-segregation-pools;

Bill Spiller:

https://www.nps.gov/nr/feature/afam/2010/Cover-AfricanAmericansinLA.pdf;

https://en.wikipedia.org/wiki/Bill_Spiller;

Billy G. Mills:

http://www.laalmanac.com/history/hi01i.php;

https://en.wikipedia.org/wiki/Billy_G._Mills;

Black Belt Jones:

https://en.wikipedia.org/wiki/Black_Belt_Jones;

Brenda Sykes:

https://achieve.lausd.net/cms/lib/CA01000043/Centricity/Domain/599/LAUSD%20Alumni%20History%20and%20Hall%20of%20Fame.pdf; (page 60);

https://en.wikipedia.org/wiki/Brenda_Sykes;

Biddy Mason:

https://www.laconser-vancy.org/locations/biddy-mason-memori-al-park ;

Buddy Collette:

https://www.allmusic.com/artist/buddy-col-lette-mn0000641450/biography

https://en.wikipedia.org/wiki/Buddy_Collette;

https://www.nps.gov/nr/feature/afam/2010/Cover-AfricanAmericansinLA.pdf

Calafia:

https://en.wikipedia.org/wiki/Calafia;

Charles Mingus:

https://www.allmusic.com/artist/charles-min-gus-mn0000009680/biography

https://en.wikipedia.org/wiki/Charles_Mingus;

https://www.nps.gov/nr/feature/afam/2010/Cover-AfricanAmericansinLA.pdf; Appendix II;

Charles Wright and the Watts 103rd Street Band:

https://www.allmusic.com/artist/charles-wright-mn0000203303/biography

https://en.wikipedia.org/wiki/Charles_Wright_%26_the_Watts_103rd_Street_Rhythm_Band;

Charlotta Bass:

https://en.wikipedia.org/wiki/Charlotta_Bass

https://www.nps.gov/nr/feature/afam/2010/Cover-AfricanAmericansinLA.pdf; Section E, page 17; Appendix II;

Chester Himes:

https://www.nps.gov/nr/feature/afam/2010/Cover-AfricanAmericansinLA.pdf

https://en.wikipedia.org/wiki/Chester_Himes;

Chester Washington:

https://en.wikipedia.org/wiki/Chester_L._Washington;

Cynthia Cooper-Dyke:

https://achieve.lausd.net/cms/lib/CA01000043/Centricity/Domain/599/LAUSD%20Alumni%20History%20and%20Hall%20of%20Fame.pdf;

https://www.wbhof.com/famers/cynthia-cooper-dyke/

Dexter Gordon:

https://www.allmusic.com/artist/dexter-gor-don-mn0000208404/biography

https://en.wikipedia.org/wiki/Dexter_Gordon;

https://www.nps.gov/nr/feature/afam/2010/Cover-AfricanAmericansinLA.pdf

Diane Watson:

https://en.wikipedia.org/wiki/Diane_Watson;

Dorothy Dandridge:

https://achieve.lausd.net/cms/lib/CA01000043/Centricity/Domain/599/LAUSD%20Alumni%20History%20and%20Hall%20of%20Fame.pdf;

Eddie 'Rochester' Anderson:

https://www.nps.gov/nr/feature/afam/2010/Cover-AfricanAmericansinLA.pdf;

https://en.wiki-pedia.org/wiki/Eddie_%22Rochester%22_Anderson;

Elvira "Vi" Redd, Jazz Saxophonist:

https://achieve.lausd.net/cms/lib/CA01000043/Centricity/Domain/599/LAUSD%20Alumni%20History%20and%20Hall%20of%20Fame.pdf; (page 178);

Etta James:

https://www.allmusic.com/artistet-ta-james-mn0000806542/biography

https://en.wikipedia.org/wiki/Etta_James;

Easy Rawlins:

https://en.wiki-pedia.org/wiki/Ezekiel_%22Easy%22_Rawlins;

Fay Allen:

https://lasentinel.net/black-women-on-lausd-board.html;

https://latimes-blogs.latimes.com/readers/2010/04/an-earlier-pioneer-on-the-la-school-board.html;

Seeking El Dorado: African Americans in California: Edited by Lawrence B de Graaf, Kevin Mulroy & Quintard Taylor. "Your Life Is Really Not Just Your Own", African American Women in Twentieth-Century California. Shirley Ann Wilson Moore. Page 220.

Ferdinand Jelly Roll Morton:

https://www.nps.gov/nr/feature/afam/2010/Cover-AfricanAmericansinLA.pdf

https://en.wikipedia.org/wiki/Jelly_Roll_Morton;

Florence Cole Talbert:

https://www.nps.gov/nr/feature/afam/2010/Cover-AfricanAmericansinLA.pdf;

https://en.wikipedia.org/wiki/Florence_Cole_Talbert;

Florence Griffith Joyner:

https://en.wikipedia.org/wiki/Florence_Griffith_Joyner;

Fred G. Sanford and His Son Lamont

https://www.imdb.com/name/nm0289359/?ref_=fn_al_nm_1

https://en.wikipedia.org/wiki/Fred_G._Sanford

Juan Francisco Reyes:

https://www.library.ucla.edu/blog/special/2015/02/26/afro-mexicans-in-early-los-angeles-exhibit-postscript#:~:text=He%20was%20both%20the%20first,now%20the%20San%20Fernando%20Valley.

https://www.blackpast.org/African American-history/reyes-juan-francisco-reyes-c-1749-c-1800/

Frederick Madison Roberts:

https://en.wikipedia.org/wiki/Frederick_Madison_Roberts;

https://www.nps.gov/nr/feature/afam/2010/Cover-AfricanAmericansinLA.pdf

Gail Smith Wyatt:

https://dorsey-lausd-ca.schoolloop.com/pf4/cms2/view_page?d=x&group_id=1537514247297&v-did=qii4e5203wpr15f;

George Bright:

https://www.lafire.com/black_ff/black.htm#:~:text=Lieutenant% 20George%20W.&text=Bright%2C%20 hired%20October%20 2%2C%201897,the%20 Los%20Angeles%20 Fire%20Department.;

The Reference Source for this section is"The LAFD Centennial 1886-1986" pages 92, 146-153 by Paul Ditzel.

https://aaregistry.org/story/the-first-black-fire-fighter-hired-in-los-angeles/;

Georgia Ann Robinson:

https://en.wikipedia.org/wiki/Georgia_Ann_Robinson#:~:text=Georgia%20Ann%20Robinson%20(n%C3%A9e%20Hill,Angeles%20Police%20Department%20(LAPD).

Gerald Wilson:

https://www.allmusic.com/artist/gerald-wilson-mn0000946171/biography

https://en.wikipedia.org/wiki/Gerald_Wilson;

Gilbert W. Lindsay:

https://en.wikipedia.org/wiki/Gilbert_W._Lindsay;

https://www.nps.gov/nr/feature/afam/2010/Cover-AfricanAmericansinLA.pdf

H. Claude Hudson:

https://www.nps.gov/nr/feature/afam/2010/Cover-AfricanAmericansinLA.pdf

https://en.wikipedia.org/wiki/H._Claude_Hudson;

Hadda Brooks:

https://en.wikipedia.org/wiki/Hadda_Brooks;

Hampton Hawes:

https://www.nps.gov/nr/feature/afam/2010/Cover-AfricanAmericansinLA.pdf;

https://en.wikipedia.org/wiki/Hampton_Hawes;

Horace Tapscott:

https://en.wikipedia.org/wiki/Horace_Tapscott;

Issa Rae:

https://en.wikipedia.org/wiki/Issa_Rae;

Ivie Anderson:

https://www.nps.gov/nr/feature/afam/2010/Cover-AfricanAmericansinLA.pdf;

https://en.wikipedia.org/wiki/Ivie_Anderson;

Jackie Lacey:

https://en.wikipedia.org/wiki/Jackie_Lacey;

James LuValle:

https://www.blackpast.org/African American-history/lu-valle-james-e-1912-1993/;

Janet Collins:

https://achieve.lausd.net/cms/lib/CA01000043/Centricity/Domain/599/LAUSD%20Alumni%20History%20and%20Hall%2oof%2oFame.pdf; (page 168);

Jessie Terry:

https://www.nps.gov/nr/feature/afam/2010/Cover-AfricanAmericansinLA.pdf;

Jody Watley:

https://dorsey-lausd-ca.schoolloop.com/pf4/cms2/view_page?d=x&group_id=1537514247297&v-did=qii4e5203wpr15f;

John J. Neimore:

https://en.wikipedia.org/wiki/California_Eagle;John_J._Neimore:

https://en.wikipedia.org/wiki/John_J._Neimore

https://www.nps.gov/nr/feature/afam/2010/Cover-AfricanAmericansinLA.pdf

John Singleton:

https://en.wikipedia.org/wiki/John_Singleton;

John Somerville:

https://www.nps.gov/nr/feature/afam/2010/Cover-AfricanAmericansinLA.pdf;

https://www.blackpast.org/African American-history/somerville-john-alexander-1882-1973/;

Johnnie Cochran:

https://en.wikipedia.org/wiki/Johnnie_Cochran;

Karen Bass:

https://en.wikipedia.org/wiki/Karen_Bass;

Kenny Washington:

https://www.britannica.com/biography/Kenny-Washington;

https://en.wikipedia.org/wiki/Kenny_Washington_(American_football);

https://www.biography.com/athlete/kenny-washington;

Leon Washington:

https://www.nps.gov/nr/feature/afam/2010/Cover-AfricanAmericansinLA.pdf;

https://en.wikipedia.org/wiki/Leon_H._Washington_Jr.;

Leonard Stovall:

https://www.nps.gov/nr/feature/afam/2010/Cover-AfricanAmericansinLA.pdf;

https://planning.lacity.org/odocument/7db8747f-87fb-4c6f-bb95-5482be050683/SurveyLA_African AmericanHCS_05242019.pdf;

Lester Young:

https://www.nps.gov/nr/feature/afam/2010/Cover-AfricanAmericansinLA.pdf;

https://en.wikipedia.org/wiki/Lester_Young;

Los Pobladores:

https://en.wikipedia.org/wiki/Los_Angeles_Pobladores;

https://www.latimes.com/archives/la-xpm-1995-02-13-me-31591-story.html;

http://www.laalmanac.com/history/hi03a.php;

Louise Beavers:

https://www.nps.gov/nr/feature/afam/2010/Cover-AfricanAmericansinLA.pdf;

https://en.wikipedia.org/wiki/Louise_Beavers;

https://www.imdb.com/name/nm0064792/?ref_=nmbio_bio_nm

Madame Sul-Te-Wan

https://www.nps.gov/nr/feature/afam/2010/Cover-AfricanAmericansinLA.pdf;

https://en.wikipedia.org/wiki/Madame_Sul-Te-Wan;

https://www.imdb.com/name/nm0837801/bio?ref_=nm_ql_1#trivia

Maggie Hathaway:

https://en.wikipedia.org/wiki/Maggie_Hathaway;

Magnificent Montague:

http://www.magnificentmontague.com/;

https://en.wikipedia.org/wiki/Magnificent_Montague;

Marguerite Justice:

https://www.latimes.com/archives/la-xpm-2009-sep-25-me-marguerite-justice25-story.html;

Marla Gibbs:

https://en.wikipedia.org/wiki/Marla_Gibbs;

https://walkoffame.com/press_releases/marlagibbs/

Mark Ridley-Thomas:

https://en.wikipedia.org/wiki/Mark_Ridley-Thomas;

https://www.latimes.com/california/story/2021-10-14/column-ridley-thomas-a-heavy-lifter-on-homelessness-now-carries-weight-of-bribery-charges;

https://www.latimes.com/california/story/2021-10-13/mark-ridley-thomas-usc-dean-bribery-indictment

https://markridley-thomas.lacity.org/articles/councilmember-ridley-thomas-celebrates-30-years-public-service-and-hosts-ribbon-cutting

https://lasentinel.net/mark-ridley-thomas-charged-along-with-former-university-dean-in-federal-grand-jury-indictment-alleging-bribery-and-fraud-scheme.html

Marvin Gaye:

https://en.wikipedia.org/wiki/Marvin_Gaye;

Maxine Waters:

https://en.wikipedia.org/wiki/Maxine_Waters;

Melba Liston:

https://achieve.lausd.net/cms/lib/CA01000043/Centricity/Domain/599/LAUSD%20Alumni%20History%20and%20Hall%20of%20Fame.pdf;

Michelle King:

https://en.wikipedia.org/wiki/Michelle_King_(educator);

http://laschoolreport.com/its-about-being-united-michelle-king-former-lausd-superintendent-who-championed-unity-dies-at-57/;

Minnie Riperton:

https://en.wikipedia.org/wiki/Minnie_Riperton;

https://www.imdb.com/name/nm0727986/bio;

Miriam Matthews:

https://en.wikipedia.org/wiki/Miriam_Matthews;

Natalie Cole:

https://en.wikipedia.org/wiki/Natalie_Cole;

Nipsey Hussle:

https://en.wikipedia.org/wiki/Nipsey_Hussle;

Norman O. Houston:

https://www.nps.gov/nr/feature/afam/2010/Cover-AfricanAmericansinLA.pdf;

https://en.wikipedia.org/wiki/Norman_O._Houston

Patrice Rushen:

https://achieve.lausd.net/cms/lib/CA01000043/Centricity/Domain/599/LAUSD%20Alumni%20History%20and%20Hall%20of%20Fame.pdf;

Paul Beatty:

https://en.wikipedia.org/wiki/Paul_Beatty;

Paul R. Williams:

https://en.wikipedia.org/wiki/Paul_R._Williams;

https://www.nps.gov/nr/feature/afam/2010/Cover-AfricanAmericansinLA.pdf;

https://achieve.lausd.net/cms/lib/CA01000043/Centricity/Domain/599/LAUSD%20Alumni%20History%20and%20Hall%20of%20Fame.pdf;

Patrisse Cullors:

https://en.wikipedia.org/wiki/Patrisse_Cullors;

Ralph Bunche:

https://www.nps.gov/nr/feature/afam/2010/Cover-AfricanAmericansinLA.pdf

(Reverend) Carl Bean aka Archbishop Carl Bean:

https://en.wikipedia.org/wiki/Carl_Bean;

https://herbwesson.com/wesson-to-honor-carl-bean-with-square-dedication/;

Richard Wyatt:

https://en.wikipedia.org/wiki/Richard_Wyatt_Jr.

https://lacontroller.org/data-stories-and-maps/African American-heritage-map/;

Rita Walters:

https://en.wikipedia.org/wiki/Rita_Walters;

Robert Owens:

https://www.nps.gov/nr/feature/afam/2010/Cover-AfricanAmericansinLA.pdf;

https://www.blackpast.org/African American-history/owens-robert-curry-1860/;

Roy Ayers:

https://en.wikipedia.org/wiki/Roy_Ayers;

Ruth Janetta Temple:

https://en.wikipedia.org/wiki/Ruth_Janetta_Temple;

Sallyanne Payton:

https://achieve.lausd.net/cms/lib/CA01000043/Centricity/Domain/599/LAUSD%20Alumni%20History%20and%20Hall%20of%20Fame.pdf; (page 59);

https://en.wikipedia.org/wiki/Sallyanne_Payton;

https://dorsey-lausd-ca.schoolloop.com/pf4/cms2/view_page?d=x&group_id=1537514247297&v-did=qii4e5203wpr15f;

Samuel Browne:

https://www.nps.gov/nr/feature/afam/2010/Cover-AfricanAmericansinLA.pdf

Susan Burton:

https://en.wikipedia.org/wiki/Susan_Burton;

Teresa Graves:

https://achieve.lausd.net/cms/lib/CA01000043/Centricity/Domain/599/LAUSD%20Alumni%20History%20and%20Hall%20of%20Fame.pdf;

https://en.wikipedia.org/wiki/Teresa_Graves;

Thomas Griffith Jr:

https://www.nps.gov/nr/feature/afam/2010/Cover-AfricanAmericansinLA.pdf

Tom Bradley:

https://en.wikipedia.org/wiki/Tom_Bradley_(American_politician);

Vada Somerville:

https://www.nps.gov/nr/feature/afam/2010/Cover-AfricanAmericansinLA.pdf

https://en.wikipedia.org/wiki/Vada_Somerville;

Valerie Brisco Hooks:

https://achieve.lausd.net/cms/lib/CA01000043/Centricity/Domain/599/LAUSD%20Alumni%20History%20and%20Hall%20of%20Fame.pdf; (page 206);

https://sports.jrank.org/
pages/620/Brisco-Hooks-
Valerie.html;

Walter Bremond:

https://brotherhoodcru-
sade.org/about-us;

Walter Mosley:

http://www.waltermos-
ley.com/;

https://en.wikipedia.org/
wiki/Walter_Mosley;

Wanda Coleman:

https://en.wikipe-
dia.org/wiki/Wanda_
Coleman#Biography;

Wendy Raquel Robinson:

https://achieve.lausd.net/
cms/lib/CA01000043/
Centricity/Domain/599/
LAUSD%20Alumni%20
History%20and%20
Hall%20of%20Fame.pdf;

https://en.wikipedia.org/
wiki/Wendy_Raquel_
Robinson;

William Grant Still:

https://www.nps.gov/nr/
feature/afam/2010/Cover-
AfricanAmericansinLA.
pdf; Appendix II; Page 11;

William Seymour:

https://www.nps.gov/nr/
feature/afam/2010/Cover-
AfricanAmericansinLA.
pdf;

https://en.wikipedia.org/
wiki/William_J._Seymour;

Woody Strode:

https://en.wikipedia.org/
wiki/Woody_Strode;

**Yvonne Brathwaite
Burke:**

https://en.wikipedia.org/
wiki/Yvonne_Brathwaite_
Burke;

INDEX

R

S

RANDAL HENRY, DRPH, MPH

EXPERT ON PUBLIC HEALTH IN LA'S PAN-AFRICAN/BLACK COMMUNITIES

(b. 1961)

Dr. Randal Henry, an expert on public health issues in LA's historically Pan-African/Black communities, is the Founding CEO of Community Intelligence, an afro-centric research and health policy consulting firm; and, the Executive Director of the Center for Healthy Neighborhoods, a non-profit working to improve health and wellbeing in under-resourced communities.

Over the course of his career, Dr. Henry encountered many people who were unaware of the contributions of African Americans to California history; the role of Afro-Latino's in the founding of Los Angeles; or, who knew nothing about African Americans from South LA except what they saw on TV or read in the newspaper. *Born in South LA* was written out of Dr. Henry's desire to help readers gain a deeper understanding of the genius and the potential of the people of South Los Angeles.

Dr. Henry was born in South LA, earned his doctorate and master of public health from University of California Los Angeles and his BA in Political Science from Cal Poly Pomona. He resides in the Crenshaw District with his beloved wife Manal and their two children, Taj and Sadiq.

KEEP IN TOUCH

 Facebook Group:
Go Crenshaw

 www.gocrenshaw.com

 @gocrenshaw

 www.gocrenshaw.shop

CPSIA information can be obtained
at www.ICGtesting.com
Printed in the USA
BVHW070228260122
627120BV00010B/879